Unmask the Invisible

An Incredible story of Faith, Family and Miracles

By

Sierra Longmoore

Bridget May

Amy Longmoore

Copyright© 2023. Sierra Longmoore Bridget May Amy Longmoore. All Rights Reserved.

No part of this work covered by the copyright herein may be reproduced or used in any form or by any means—graphic, electronic, or mechanical without the prior written permission of the publisher. Any request for photocopying, recording, taping, or information storage and retrieval systems of any part of this book shall be directed in writing to the author.

This publication contains the opinions and ideas of its author(s) and is designed to provide useful advice in regard to the subject matter covered.

Acknowledgments... With Our Deepest Gratitude

When your family experiences something as devastating as a teen being in a catastrophic car crash, it sends everyone into a state of shock of varying degrees. The news, and then the not knowing, and then the sinking in of reality, are all traumatic to deal with. You don't know what to do or how to do it. It's like the ground opens and drops out from under you.

I cannot, in good faith, begin without acknowledgment of the power of God and St. Padre Pio. With divine guidance, love, and spiritual support, we can fight the toughest battles. And we have witnessed Sierra be the one most divinely influenced journey through all of this.

Having the right people be on duty or driving past at the right time is integral to the survival of the person involved, not just the trained professionals but the compassionate first-on-scene bystanders who also contribute in immeasurable ways. Their kindness will never be forgotten. As family members, your only focus is discovering information. Are they OK? How bad is it? And then, when will you see them smile or laugh again? Will they walk again? Will they live as they had before?

We would like to take this opportunity to express our deepest gratitude to all the people who have contributed to Sierra's healing journey. From the moment the crash happened, God put the right person in place at the right time, and we are thankful.

Words cannot express our deepest appreciation to the twenty-three people first on the scene: the bystanders who arrived within seconds of her car leaving the road, who picked up her belongings, called 911, and spoke love over her, the state trooper, and the emergency service responders:

Dan Martin	Melanie Minshull
Bill Kearney	John Renfrew
Stacie Peyrat	Wally Fischer
Jennifer Dube	Gordon Huntington
Jacob Dube	Harrison Renfrew
Jason Haley	Jack Palmer
Riley Harness	DHART Ethan Ballin
Nate Brooks	Pilot Doug Moore
Rachel Harness	RN Caleb Moffat
Bob Taylor	Jeremiah Goyette
Steve Robbins	Jeremy Patten
Dick Guy	

We are deeply indebted to the E.R. and PICU staff, doctors, surgeons, nurses, therapists, and clergy at Dartmouth–Hitchcock Medical Center, especially the following people:

Rev. Samuel Seyd (Father Sam) became our spiritual pillar of strength at Dartmouth-Hitchcock.

The head Pediatric Intensive Care Unit doctor (PICU), Dr. Braga, and the head nurse, Kathleen, whose kindness was generous and appreciated, as well as PICU nurses Chloe, Sarah, Leah, Charlie, and Sean.

Dr. John Kanter, Dr. Perry Ball, Dr. Patricia Clerkin, and their support teams.

We would also like to thank the Dartmouth Hitchcock Medical Center (DHMC) therapists: Danielle, Maxwell, and Jen.

We are extremely grateful to the team at Spaulding Rehabilitation Hospital in Boston, whose enthusiasm and dedication to their Pediatric patients brought more strength to our family in those dark moments than we knew we needed: Nurses Megan, Teresa, Rachel, and Nancy, and therapists Michelle, Victoria and Francesca along with other supporting staff, lifted us more often than they realized.

We cannot begin to express our overwhelming gratitude to The Home Depot family, who showered us with such an outpouring of support and love we were often momentarily lifted from the pain we were experiencing. Steven would like to especially thank The Home Depot leadership and associates of the company for their support and love throughout this journey. Special thanks to those who contributed their personal testimonies, including:

Jason Aragoni   John Carr

Chrissy Roberts   Lisa Beam

Our sincere appreciation to Jerry Serra for his commitment and time to beta-read the draft book.

I'd like to acknowledge our community of prayer warriors, locally led by Father Andrew and our home church community of Our Lady of Perpetual Help, who immediately started praying for us and Sierra.

I'd also like to acknowledge the wisdom and knowledge shared by the mothers whose children had also experienced T.B.I. Without their gracious sharing of knowledge, so much of this journey would have been much more difficult to navigate.

We are grateful for Jim Kenyon from Valley News and Amy Ash Nixon of the Caledonia News; their reporting and opinion pieces were well written and greatly appreciated in bringing people accurate news of Sierra's progress.

The outstanding support from Oxbow High School – the Counseling Coordinator, Lomond Richardson, whose support in acting as a source of information for people was incredible and helped us so much.

A massive Thank You to Mrs. Leddy, who devoted so much to tutoring Sierra. We are deeply grateful.

The local community – the local businesses and sports teams who proudly displayed their #SierraStrong signs and symbols of support from the local youth baseball team to the local speedway, the nurse from DHMC who made us all angel charms, the people who sold bracelets and t-shirts and who fundraised to support us, we will never forget the incredible displays of support demonstrated by all these people. They carried us further than they will ever know.

We would like to say thank you for the gifts of assistance from local businesses:

Youngs Photography, Newbury, Vermont.

Robert Charles Photography, East Longmeadow, Massachusetts.

Lance and Melissa Battersby from The Newbury Village Store.

The Upper Valley Aquatic Center, White River Junction, Vermont.

Nadina Pitaro and Epidavoras Day Spa, Mount Kisco, New York.

Nicole Chase from Belleza Hair Salon, West Lebanon, New Hampshire.

Andrea Covey with Pheonix Rizing Guides, Newbury, Vermont.

The Gladstone Family from Fairlee, VT.

The therapists, trainers, and coaches who treated Sierra with such faith and inspiration:

Joey Farley with R.E.P Fitness

Gretchen Moulton with Gretchen Moulton, L.L.C.

Lori Ramalho with Light Insights

As well as the wide variety of therapies that have made a difference in Sierra's healing, some of which we were unfamiliar with at the start but made such a difference:

Acupuncture	Stem Cell Therapy
Creative Art Therapy	Biomagnetism
Hyperbaric Oxygen Therapy	Neurofeedback
Design for Strong Minds	

The support we received from the "Miracle for Sierra – God's Heroes Unite" Facebook page was also beyond expectation; we are grateful for the love and support from so many people from all over the world. The unconditional friendship and support from people like Walter Way have given us the richness of new family friends.

Our extended family members and especially Steven's parents, Steve and Denise, without whom everything would have been much more difficult. Their selfless dedication to being there for our other children, feeding us, and being available at all hours of the day and night really gives depth to the unconditional love of family.

And lastly, I would like to acknowledge Sierra's siblings:

Tristan, Lindsay, Aspen, and Tanner stepped up in countless ways. All maturing far too quickly under such stressful circumstances but supporting and loving each other and us through the trauma of Sierra's injury. A parent's heart and love are equal and unconditional, but seeing the way all our children pulled together to support each other and us, their parents, has made me feel like my heart is ten times bigger and filled with such pride and fullness knowing we have raised such thoughtful, caring, compassionate, strong and all-around great humans.

With Love-

Steven and Amy

Table of Contents

Introduction 11

Chapter One – Unrecognizable Pieces 17

Chapter Two – The First 24 Hours 28

Chapter Three – Dartmouth Hitchcock Medical Center 37

Chapter Four – Sierra at Spaulding 58

Chapter Five – Tides Turn 85

Chapter Six – One Day at a Time 100

Chapter Seven – Love Is Action 116

Chapter Eight – Warrior Spirit 127

Chapter Nine – Spiritual Revelations 142

Chapter Ten – Our Orange Family 156

Chapter Eleven - Milestones 168

Chapter Twelve – Transformational Strength 184

Chapter Thirteen – Blessings 200

Chapter Fourteen – Joyful Seasons 216

Chapter Fifteen – A Foundation Is Born 232

Chapter Sixteen – Love Wins 241

Introduction

BUT THOSE WHO WAIT ON THE LORD
Shall renew their strength.
They will soar on wings like eagles;
they will run and not grow weary,
they will walk and not be faint.

Isaiah 40:31 (NVKJ)

In the summer of 2020, our entire family changed forever. At just seventeen years old, our oldest twin, Sierra, fell victim to a car crash. She did not suffer any internal injuries or major broken bones, but she did experience multiple skull fractures and a massive severe traumatic brain injury. Given the circumstances, she should have died that day.

Many parts of her brain were shredded, her spinal cord ruptured, she had four separate fractures around the circumference of her skull, she stopped breathing, and there was zero oxygen in her system as she was airlifted to a local hospital. My husband and eldest son rushed to the scene of the crash and did not think there was a way anyone could have survived.

As a Catholic family of deep faith, we know that God has a plan for each of us who walk the earth as his precious and favored children. Even though it was a very tumultuous time, our instinct from that very moment was to pray to our Almighty

Father. Anyone who believes in Jesus Christ knows that the power of prayer is real and incredible.

From then on, we witnessed miracle after miracle. The fact that she even made it to the hospital alive was miracle number one. As the hours turned into days, we were shown signs and messages that God and his army were with us as Sierra fought for her life. We had people telling us to pray to the patron saint of suffering and healing, Padre Pio.

He has a reputation for making himself known on a spiritual level and in all sorts of seemingly random occurrences when he can be of assistance to a person. This took on greater significance later in Sierra's story.

There were many pivotal moments in her journey of survival when the right person was placed in our path to do or say the right thing. There were too many coincidences to ignore, and there was no doubt we were being divinely guided.

The support that lifted us, coming from all areas of our lives, was nothing short of incredible. It was deeply comforting to know we were not alone. Spiritually or physically.

Through it all, we continued to believe she would live; she would be delivered back to us. Even during the times we could not understand what was happening, there was never a time that we doubted her return.

After surrendering Sierra's journey to God, trusting that he would put qualified people, treatment options, knowledge, and therapies in front of us as they were required, we stopped questioning His plan. We met or were referred to many people who are trained or very experienced in the metaphysical and alternative realms.

This has also been a learning process for us, but through it all, we have learned to let God take these things we have no control over. We have seen His grace multiple times. He oversees everything.

In the following pages, I share with you the incredible journey against insurmountable odds that Sierra has undertaken and how it has affected hundreds, if not thousands, of people, bringing them back to God.

The support we received was incredible and even surreal at times. I believe that with all the isolation many people faced due to COVID restrictions in their day-to-day lives, her journey brought so many people together online with a joint sense of community. Many friendships were built from that time and remain today.

Sierra's story is also a testament to the strength of our strong family ties, with our extended family surrounding us in a spiritual circling of the wagons. This journey has changed every single one of us in ways we never imagined. It is adversity that shapes us, either by being faced, thereby making us stronger and more courageous, or by running away and causing fracture and discourse of both characters and situations.

I am hesitant to share the rest of the story. The one about her ex, who emotionally and physically abused her, gave her a black eye and threatened her after they broke up. The story is about how she was too scared to tell us about the behavior she was subjected to, as she believed him when he told her he was the only one who would ever love her.

When she broke up with him in a moment of clarity, his attempts at emotional blackmail, which had worked before, had lost its power over her, and she was done. It was summer, and she was looking forward to getting away for our annual vacation at the beach.

This culminated in him telling her he would kill her the morning of her crash and weeks after the crash. An eyewitness came forward who reported seeing a car matching the ex's friend following Sierras very closely on the morning of the crash on the curvy, steep road close to our home. The memory remained in the eyewitness's memory, which was shared with me at a pivotal point in the journey.

I have also been hesitant to share his behavior since the crash, the continual harassment of our family, joined often by his friends. His periodic trespassing and the attempts to intimidate and stalk us. Never knowing when some lost soul might show up on your doorstep is unnerving, to say the least.

All this despite the restraining orders and orders of protection, combined with the formal litigation to stop his deranged behavior, which has gone on for years. Battling all of this behind the scenes as we fought for our daughter to survive while protecting our other children and family members from these random acts of violence.

Witnessing first-hand the lack of protection offered to the victims of bullying and domestic violence cases has made our family huge supporters of anti-bullying and proponents of domestic violence education. Even though the perpetrator somehow believes that his desire to be in Sierra's life should be enforced, we continue to pray for him. We want to exist in a place of forgiveness. What we hope for in this world, we must create. Through forgiveness, we enhance the presence of compassion in the world.

We know that God sees all. He knows who has wronged who, and at the end of a life, what is in one's heart is something to be discussed with God. Not us. It is not for our family to seek revenge, be consumed with fear or rage, or pass judgment on this person. We believe once a heart has turned to thoughts of revenge, the enemy has already won. We choose to receive God's blessings and leave Him to do the balancing of the scales.

Our focus is the joy and favor God has blessed our family with. The miracles he has bestowed on Sierra. It is our role to spread love, not hate. As we now help others and support those in need the way we were once supported (and still are), we know that we are on the right path.

We have been divinely and physically supported and uplifted. Sierra has survived the un-survivable. Her warrior spirit and determination have inspired all who know her, as well as those who did not know her before. God saves his toughest battles for his strongest warriors, and I have seen this to be true. Physical strength has nothing on the strength of hearts, minds, and prayer.

It is our hope that by sharing her story, we can offer support and inspiration to others experiencing difficult circumstances. Sierra has returned to us as an extremely compassionate and loving person, and it has been her deepest desire to help others who are experiencing similar situations as her own.

We support her fully in this, and we have helped her launch an organization to raise awareness and support members of our communities experiencing "the invisible" challenges in life. Traumatic brain injuries, domestic violence, respite care, and sibling support are all under the name of "Unmask the Invisible."

Although this future was never considered or imagined before 2020, I have learned that God has a bigger plan, and we have faith in his direction. God is in control, not us. He speaks to us through people who are in the right place at the right time, through signs, nature, and dreams; we just have to notice.

I've learned people's true character and strength shine through in the worst of circumstances. Complete strangers can make a profound impact on our lives. There are no guarantees in life, and to trust in God's process.

This is Sierra's story....

Chapter One – Unrecognizable Pieces

[26] My flesh and my heart fail;
But God *is* the strength of my heart and my portion forever.
Psalms 73:26

"Where there is great love, there are always miracles."

- Willa Cather

Wednesday, July 8th, 2020, started like almost every other summer morning for our family of seven. Although spirits were high and there was an air of anticipation, later that day, we were heading to Maine for our annual family vacation at the beach, and we could not have felt happier.

Complete with the annual group picture, it had been a family tradition for years, an extended family trip with cousins and their families. This year, we even made matching t-shirts that said: "Life is better around the campfire – Longmoore Adventure 2020".

We had worried for months that we would not be able to take the trip. The COVID-19 pandemic had been out of control and kept everyone at home and isolated for months, which was unlike anything anyone had experienced before.

We discovered just a few weeks before, in June, that restrictions had been lifted for the oceanside campground we frequented and were excited to know we could still go. There were still obviously restrictions in place, but we were happy to social distance or abide by whatever rules were set. The camper was already hooked up to Steven's truck.

We had planned to take the boys in the early afternoon, and the girls would follow later after they had all finished work. This vacation was just what our family needed: to decompress, get away from our house, which we had spent a whole lot of time in, and return to our familiar summer tradition.

Lindsay, our eldest daughter, our twins Aspen and Sierra, and I had all left within thirty minutes of each other after breakfast to head to our prospective workplaces. Sierra had left the house last, only needing to drive a few miles to her babysitting job.

My husband Steven and our two boys were still at home. Steven made himself a coffee and was out on the deck when the doorbell rang. Curious about who could be at the door at 8:30 in the morning, he opened it and saw an unfamiliar man on the doorstep.

He had our daughter's driver's license in his hand and said his name was Bill. He held it out to Steven and asked if he was Sierra's father.

Steven nodded, wondering why Bill had it, and reaching to take the license from Bill's outstretched hand, he asked nervously. "Is everything OK? Where's Sierra?"

Bill looked at him grimly, eyes wide as he shook his head very slightly and informed him that Sierra had been in a crash on Snake Road, just a couple of miles from our home.

Bill lived on Snake Road and had heard the crash as he was eating breakfast. The ugly, violent sound of metal crunching, the heavy bouncing of a vehicle flipping and trees creaking and foliage breaking, and then disconcerting silence.

He knew immediately that someone had left the road. As he ran downhill towards the sound, Bill tried dialing 911 on his mobile phone with no luck. Frustrated he had no signal, he could see Stacie, another neighbor, at the mangled wreck of the vehicle. She, too, had heard the unmistakable sound of a vehicle rolling over and crashing and was the first to arrive, living just across the road.

"Have you called 911?" he shouted, flustered.

"I have no signal!" Stacie had also tried but had no service either.

She kept trying, equally as frustrated. Just then, Jennifer pulled up. She could see the vehicle mangled and smashed against the tree and the trail of debris all over the road, and realizing this just happened, she leaped out of her car to help. Bill decided to run home to call 911 from his landline.

Jennifer could see the driver was unconscious as she dashed over to the vehicle. She realized she was just a teenager and automatically reached into the window to comfort the young woman. She didn't want her to feel alone, and she started speaking, saying the words that came to her, "Your family is coming," "You're so strong," "I'm so proud of you," words of reassurance and comfort. Jennifer didn't know Sierra, but she did know this young woman needed some strong words of encouragement and love spoken over her.

As Bill got back to the scene, another car had stopped, and the driver and passenger were picking up Sierra's personal belongings and the contents of the vehicle. In doing so, they found her driver's license. Bill didn't recognize our family name but was familiar with the road we lived on. Knowing it was the right thing to do, he got in his car and headed to our address.

Steven could tell from the man's demeanor that it was a serious crash.

"It's about a mile up Snake Road, I'll show you," Bill offered.

Steven nodded, and he yelled urgently for our oldest son, Tristan, who was still in bed, "Get your keys! We gotta go!"

Tristan, who was just waking up, had never heard his dad use that alarmed tone of voice before and was dressed and downstairs in a flash. A minute later, they bolted out the door and hastily drove to the horrific scene.

Snake Road is an infamous sharp and curvy road that forces drivers to the minimum speed limit due to its multiple tight curves. On a map, it looks like a giant snake winding across the land, hence its name.

As they drove together, it felt like it took forever to reach the scene. They made the journey in silence. Both felt apprehensive about what they were going to see. Both had a sense of impending doom.

The SUV Sierra had been driving looked like a crumpled white tin can wrapped around the trunk of a tall oak tree that stood firm despite the impact. The massive tree was missing a huge chunk of bark where the vehicle had hit, leaving a huge ugly gash to the young sapwood beneath, and debris was everywhere. Sierra's belongings were ejected from the vehicle and laid all over the road with broken glass and pieces of the SUV scattered like birdseed.

By the time Steven and Tristan arrived at the crash scene, almost two dozen people were spread out around the large oak tree where the white SUV was crumpled like a piece of foil. There were EMS vehicles, fire, police, and the first on-scene drivers and passengers.

It was shocking to realize our precious daughter had been inside. The number of emergency vehicles and flashing lights was overwhelming. Steven and Tristan surveyed the scene as they were approached by State Trooper Haley, who offered to take

Steven to the ambulance where Sierra was. Steven felt trepidation but knew he had to see his daughter.

Trooper Haley put his arm around him and guided him gently towards the ambulance. Telling him to just stay with him and that it would be tough. Tristan stood there dazed and in shock, trying to comprehend what he was seeing.

As Steven and Trooper Haley approached the ambulance, Steven saw Sierra in there. He could see the EMTs working on her. She was breathing very hard, and he was struck by two things – overwhelming relief that she was alive, which instantly gave him hope, and the frantic faces of the EMTs working on stabilizing her for transport. My husband describes it as one of the worst moments of his life. The image burned into his memory forever.

Tristan was equally shocked when he surveyed the scene. His little sister, the car, the tree, debris all over the road, the looks on the faces of all the people who were helping; he felt there was no way Sierra survived. His heart dropped, as all the air had just been sucked out of him, making him feel simultaneously numb and dead inside, sure a pivotal piece of our family was lost.

Steven and Tristan were advised to head to Dartmouth Hitchcock Hospital and to alert the rest of the family. Steven nodded in shock, still trying to process what he was seeing. There were so many people working on her, so many tubes, and she looked so small. He didn't want to leave, but he told her he loved her and he would see her soon.

In the ambulance, EMTs could not find any oxygen saturation levels in Sierra's blood. She had severe traumatic brain injury pulmonary contusions and was in a near-brain-dead state. There was spinal fluid leaking out of her left ear, and she was completely unresponsive. They inserted a breathing tube immediately as she was having trouble breathing on her own.

The emergency helicopter was delayed by the tall trees and the narrow winding road, which made it impossible to land safely, forcing them to land in a nearby field. Traffic had been stopped in both directions and by the time Sierra arrived at the hospital, the golden hour had passed. There were strong signs that she was still there, and nobody was ready to give up on her yet.

The subsequent police investigation determined that the vehicle had left the road at great speed, flying approximately thirteen feet into the air and flipping three times before being forcefully stopped by smashing into an oak tree.

The driver's side took the brunt of the impact, and several airbags, including the steering wheel, did not deploy. Sierra had been wearing her seatbelt, which had kept her in place, thereby preventing major bodily trauma, but her head had taken the brunt of the impact. Little did we know until forty days later that we discovered that the speed was a result of her driving to escape someone chasing her.

I was working at a client's office when I received a call from Steven saying Sierra was in a crash. But that was all I heard.

The reception was terrible, and the call dropped. How bad could it be? I thought to myself, maybe she hit someone's fender or tapped a guardrail. My phone rang again. This time, Steven was crying, telling me it was bad and she was being airlifted to the nearby hospital.

My insides dropped, replaced by a vice-like feeling gripping my chest. I could not breathe. I could not fathom what I had just heard. I did not know if I was going to be sick or start crying. My client looked concerned as I stammered my apologies, grabbed my belongings, and hurried to the hospital.

Our oldest daughter, Lindsay, worked nearby at a retirement community. She was with a patient when I called her. She knew I would not bother her at work unless it was an emergency. When she answered, I could not speak; all she could hear was me crying, and she knew things were not OK.

She had a tough time understanding what I was trying to tell her, but through my tears and near hysteria, I managed to tell her that Sierra was in a terrible crash and was being airlifted to Dartmouth Hitchcock Hospital. Lindsay was speechless.

"I'm on my way, Mom," was all she said, and she immediately left work to meet me at the hospital.

Next, I called our youngest daughter, Aspen, Sierra's fraternal twin. I told her Sierra was in a serious crash, and she had to get to the hospital as soon as possible. I was worried about her safety, thinking she might speed just to get there as soon as she could.

As she drove, Aspen spoke to Sierra in her head, repeating, "I'm coming, Sierra," over and over. One exit away from the hospital, Aspen was pulled over by a State Trooper in an unmarked car. He saw Aspen was extremely upset, and when she told him why she was in such a hurry, he already knew the details, having heard it on his radio, and offered her an escort to guide her safely to the hospital. Aspen felt even more upset. If a State Trooper knew about the crash, it must be really bad.

Tristan and Steven were also escorted to the hospital. Tristan dropped Steven at the hospital and then headed back home to pick up our youngest son, Tanner, who still did not know that his sister had been in a crash. Time was of the essence, but it also stood still, as time often does in times of intense emotional trauma. We were all paralyzed with fear and shock, feeling like we were floating outside of our bodies. Only about 40 minutes had passed since Bill knocked on our door.

As we waited, I could not keep still. I paced anxiously up and down the hallway of the emergency waiting room, praying to God to spare Sierra's life and asking my mom's spirit to hold her hand as I could not.

My mother had passed away a few years before and had always immensely loved the twins. She delighted in "double the joy" when they were toddlers. I knew she would be watching out for Sierra right now. Lindsay immediately started calling the family to let them know what happened. We are blessed with a large extended family, and it was her instinct to let them know and ask them to start praying.

Everyone arrived seemingly at the same time, including extended family members, Steven's parents, as well as uncles and cousins. We were all together when the helicopter landed. They told us they were rushing her straight to have a CAT scan first.

Nobody saw her, and they didn't tell us much else. By this point, we had been moved to a private room. I did not know if it was for discretion because we were loud and upset or because there were just so many of us.

Aspen was inconsolable. She texted her boyfriend who immediately came to the hospital to offer support to Aspen as he knew how close they were. We could not see what was going on behind the scenes; there were no immediate answers, and it felt like a lifetime had passed as we waited for details. We held hands and began to pray.

We did not know how serious her injuries were if she was still unconscious, or if she was paralyzed, we did not know anything. We also did not know when we would be told anything; it was awful. We were told the on-duty Chaplin would be joining us. This was somewhat reassuring, and we were looking forward to the hospital Chaplin being with us.

There were twelve of us in the tiny 4 x 8 room, sitting and standing, holding hands and with our arms around each other. Just waiting. As the Chaplin entered the room, she looked unsure of herself. We all stopped, looking at her expectantly to tell us what she knew.

She introduced herself and took a deep breath as she looked around at us all and told us that she had just seen Sierra as she was wheeled into the ICU. She let out a deep breath in a halted, shuddery way and started crying. She did not need to tell us that things did not look good. Just the fact that she was so visibly shaken said everything her words did not. She prayed with us, and after she left, we continued to pray.

We prayed to stop any other thoughts from entering our heads, concentrating on Sierra in that tiny room. Not wanting to entertain any other thoughts except the wish to see her smile and laugh again. I thought I would go crazy with anxiety, and we still did not know how the crash even happened or the extent of her injuries. The only thing that kept me grounded was praying with our family.

Chapter Two – The First 24 Hours

> 13 So now faith, hope, and love abide, these three; but the greatest of these is love. 1 Corinthians 13:13

We did not say anything except the prayers. All of us were lost in our thoughts of the last time we each saw Sierra, our daughter, sister, cousin, niece, or grandchild. Full of life and spirit, we prayed fervently for her survival. Aspen was inconsolable, but her sobs somehow pulled us together in unity.

After what felt like forever, they were done with her CT scan, X-rays, and other tests, and we were able to go into the emergency room and see her, but only two at a time due to COVID restrictions.

Steven and I went in first. When I saw her, hot tears filled my eyes and blurred my vision. I felt sick to my stomach, wishing I could trade places with her. I wanted to run over and scoop her up, but she was hooked up to so many beeping machines, a breathing tube, and a drip. She had IVs in both of her arms, and both hands. Above her head was a monitor with all her vitals, which updated every few seconds.

Her head was completely bandaged, with only part of her face visible. There were all sorts of devices strapped to her head protruding from the bandages, including a bolt drilled into the top of her skull to monitor her brain pressure.

Both of her lungs had collapsed from the intense pressure of her body coming to a sudden stop, and she was not breathing on her own. There was a port in her chest, too, and she had been placed in a medically induced coma to preserve a controlled state of unconsciousness to stop the damage in her brain from progressing as it tried to heal itself.

Often, in the case of severe brain injury from a crash like Sierra's, as the brain tries to recover, the consequences become life-threatening, and the only way to mitigate this is to shut it down with powerful sedative-hypnotic drugs to induce anesthesia, thereby giving the body a chance to heal.

We could barely hold her hands with tubes and IVs everywhere. It was incredibly overwhelming. Steven and I both cried and told her we loved her and we were all right there for her. I knew she could hear us; I knew she was still in there.

As we proceeded back to the waiting room, our family members could read our pulverized body language and grieving facial expressions, which spoke to how dire the circumstances were.

Aspen and Lindsay were next to visit Sierra. Aspen was so distraught she could hardly speak and could not believe what she was seeing; her eyes were as big as saucers transfixed on her twin, horrified as she tried to take it all in.

It was the first time in seventeen and a half years that something terrible had happened to either one of them. She just held on to what she could of Sierra's hand and cried. Lindsay is a very emotionally strong person. As the eldest sister, she knew the twins (and Tanner) looked up to her and Tristin as the big kids.

She was always so compassionate with them; this time, it was no different. She was Aspen's rock as they prayed and spoke to Sierra together, telling her they loved her and that she needed to come home. A nurse gave them Sierra's bracelet, which Aspen hung on to for a while before giving it to Steven, intuitively feeling that her dad needed it more. Sierra was always her dad's girl. Tagging along with him, hunting and fishing from an early age.

Two by two family members retreated to a room in the ER to visit Sierra. Everyone was still in shock; we couldn't fathom the injuries or what we were about to hear.

A neurologist who introduced himself as Dr. Dan met with us back in the tiny private room. He looked tired and serious but retained a professional expression so as not to give away his own feelings regarding the news he was about to deliver. He brought in a laptop on a stand with wheels that we gathered around as he did his best to simplify the injuries Sierra had suffered in this "severe traumatic brain injury."

Until that point in life, we did not know what that meant. Sure, we had heard of brain injuries, but like so many things, until it affects your family, you are in the dark. As he spoke, the walls pressed in even further.

He started by explaining as simply as he could what happened to Sierra in the crash. How the left side of her head had hit the tree, and her face hit the steering wheel, breaking her teeth. The blunt force trauma had caused both of her lungs to collapse.

She suffered four fractures around the circumference of her skull, one severing her facial nerve on the left side, and there was severe damage to what seemed like every area of her brain, including her brain stem. At the crash scene, she had spinal fluid and blood streaming out of her left ear.

She was diagnosed with Diffuse Axonal Injury (DAI) at the scene, which is the tearing of the brain's long connecting nerve fibers, which caused a lack of oxygen to her brain. When the body comes to a sudden stop, the brain has enough room in the skull so that it slams into the front and then ricochets into the back of the head, often twisting at the same time. The amount of time she was without oxygen had caused her to suffer a stroke mid-brain.

As he matter-of-factly shared the information, he pointed to the bright white areas on the CT scan of her brain with his pen on the laptop screen. This was where she had bleeding in the space between the brain and the tissue covering the brain.

Then, pointing to another area, that was where there was blood along the falx and tentorium, at the part of the brain that separates part of the cerebrum (which is the largest part of the brain and is divided into two hemispheres) from the cerebellum (which is the portion of the brain in the back of the head) that controls balance for walking and standing and other complex motor functions.

There was also massive damage to the part that connected to the brain stem and constrained brain motion. This part separates both sides of the brain and is stiffer than other parts of the brain, which is particularly important in transferring information within the brain. He took a breath as he looked at us and went on.

She had a severed bilateral temporal bone with fractures that extended into the middle ear cavity, which is one of the most complex bones of the body. Surrounding the ear canal and protecting the temporal lobe, it is the area of the brain believed to play a role in processing language/auditory information, emotions, visual perception, and encoding memory.

There was a mid-brain bleed, which disrupted the oxygen flow within the brain that they were concerned about, as it often leads to tissue death. There was also a fracture line across the base of her skull, through the bony part of her cranium at the very top on the left side near the artery that rises directly from the heart, which is the primary source of oxygenated blood to the head and neck.

The parts of her bony brain plates that connect to each other like mini fringes had separated where they met on both sides. There was bleeding in the right temple area of the brain, which is the part that processes non-verbal memory.

Our heads were spinning, attempting to understand all this information. It did not sound good. It did not look good. The image he was showing us didn't look good at all. There were bright white areas of damage all over the place.

He paused, quickly scanning our faces, and taking a deep breath in, he gently asked, "Would you like me to go on?"

I do not think any of us moved. We were all too stunned to fully comprehend what he was telling us. Although I had been desperately praying for her life, I had not believed that she could die. Not our Sierra. She was our fighter. God had other plans for her. For a moment, I was not so sure. I just felt disbelief. There must be a mistake; this cannot be our daughter's scan. There must have been another teenage girl who was in a car crash, and they got their charts confused.

Dr. Dan told us that they were deeply concerned about the length of time her brain had lacked oxygen during the critical time after the accident and that it would severely impact her body's ability to heal the parts of her brain that had suffered the most.

He briefly outlined the rest of the damage and, taking another deep breath, told us that her prognosis was not good. He did not expect her to make it through the night. Everything stopped at that moment. It was as if someone had ripped the soul and spirit out of our bodies and fastened heavyweights to our feet. We could not move; it was hard to breathe. He went on to tell us that they were trying to stabilize her through life support and were moving her to a private room in the Pediatric Intensive Care Unit (PICU).

It was there in the PICU room where we met the other teams who would work to save Sierra. There were teams from

Trauma, Neurology, Pediatric Critical Care, Respiratory and Radiology. Steven will never forget the words of one of the Radiologists who conducted the initial CT scan.

"Right now, we are not focused on her recovery, just survival. We do not expect anything beyond that." Those words paralyzed us.

We were devastated, but we did not stop praying. Steven and I sat vigil at her bedside, praying for divine intervention to heal our daughter and bring her home. The family members who had been with us all day left and were rallying prayer warriors and letting people know we needed a miracle for Sierra.

As always, though, in situations of a dire emergency involving someone you know, people have varied reactions and true colors become apparent.

Sierra's ex-boyfriend (she broke up with him a couple of days before the accident after discovering his infidelity) was very urgently trying to gain access to her, trying to find out what she remembered. It was strangely obsessive, not the usual grief you would expect when someone just found out about a terrible crash.

He was frantic, calling our phones and sending dozens of messages to all family members, as well as messaging through social media. He managed to get into the emergency room, and Steven saw him skirting the periphery of the ward.

Steven approached him and spoke to him briefly. He was struck by how strange it was that his demeanor was not sad or concerned. It was more like he was just wanting information. The first thing he told Steven was where he had been that morning.

Steven had no idea what this kid was trying to achieve and put it down to shock. Sierra had told her dad that they broke up because he had cheated on her, and Steven was not interested in consoling his daughter's ex-boyfriend, especially when he did not even ask how she was doing.

We later discovered he had called Sierra's phone multiple times that day, too. Although odd, the significance barely registered until later. It was all lost in the noise. Our worry and prayers for Sierra were by far the most important thing.

We knew, without a doubt, that if Sierra were to survive, only God could do the impossible. Until that day, every memory I had of the Dartmouth Hitchcock Medical Center was joyous. Until then, I associated the hospital with childbirth and the incredible blessings of our five beautiful children. Even when the twins were born prematurely, we were confident in the ability of the doctors and nurses working so hard to give our girls the best chance to thrive.

This time was certainly different. The disruptive force that made time stand still and threw our lives into turmoil with just one phone call gave us an entirely new perspective of the hospital. As the first day turned into the first night turned into the first few days, Steven and I did not leave.

As a Catholic family, we have strong faith, and as this unfolded, we became stronger together, each knowing the role we needed to take to continue life in some capacity of normal. Lindsay and Tristan immediately took control of our home, taking care of the pets and Tanner.

Somehow, every care in the world disappeared from our minds – work, bills, managing the household, appointments, upcoming celebrations – everything took a backseat to the present moment.

Chapter Three – Dartmouth Hitchcock Medical Center

[27] Peace I leave with you, My peace I give to you; not as the world gives do I give to you. Let not your heart be troubled, neither let it be afraid. John 14:27

Time tends to become distorted in hospitals, both slowing down and speeding up at the same time. For family members desperately waiting at the bedside for improvement in a loved one, time is suspended.

Steven and I did not sleep for four days; neither of us could leave Sierra while she remained suspended between life and death with no change in her condition. Aspen stayed for as long as possible. She could not bear to leave her twin. Sierra was very still, and she looked tiny in the middle of all the tubes, machines, and wires.

At times, we needed to move away and take a break somewhere quiet. We were overwhelmed by the equipment keeping her alive, which surrounded her like a diligent army. The IV pump hummed, her ventilator clicked and whispered as it pushed air into her lungs, the vital signs monitor consistently beeped while continually measuring her blood pressure, oxygen saturation, temperature, and heart rate, and the intracranial brain pressure monitors quietly beeped as well.

Occasionally, one machine would sound an alert, and a nurse would be in the room in seconds to tend to the issue. There was a constant flow of nurses and doctors entering and leaving. When it just got too much, Steven and I would take turns retreating to the quiet of the hospital chapel.

Sierra's condition was not improving. She was just in limbo. We were sure she was still there and would hold her lifeless hands and pray continually for God to bring her back to us.

The staff were very respectful and worked around us when they had to tend to Sierra. Two nurses lovingly took hours to wash the blood from Sierra's hair. They were so gentle and reverent that I was touched by their actions. Still, we prayed. Steven and I did not leave her bedside; one of us was always right there with her.

There were not supposed to be more than two people with Sierra at any time, but the head nurse, Kathleen, had compassion for us, letting Aspen stay with Sierra, too. We later discovered Kathleen had also given birth to her daughter in the same NICU just days before the twins were born in 2002. She recognized the twin bond and could not bear to separate them.

Our two eldest children, Tristan and Lindsay, took care of Tanner, our youngest. And all three of them took care of the house and our three dogs and three cats. One of Sierra's cats did not leave his spot on her bed for any longer than the time it took to eat and use the litter box, and then he would return quickly, waiting for her to come home. Lindsay and Tristan were incredible, quickly becoming the point of contact for the whole family and taking the pressure off us.

She and Tristan also took care of everything around the house, fielding phone calls from people we knew through high school, sports, church, work, and the community in general from all the activities our family participated in. So many were calling for updates and wanting to know what they could do. Family members and friends delivered meals to Steven's parents' house; people were so kind that it was overwhelming, and although it barely registered, we were numb. All we asked for was prayers for a miracle for Sierra.

What started as a trickle quickly became a flood, and it was about then that we started to become aware of the love and support that was being directed towards us. As news of the crash traveled rapidly, at the hospital, our phones were continually vibrating with phone calls and messages from people sending prayers and love, letting us know that we were not alone.

It felt like a soft, supportive blanket, energetically surrounding us. Flowers, cards, and gifts flooded Sierra's hospital room. It certainly was wonderful to receive such positive energy, and I read every single card and message, although, as I came to realize later, because we were so emotionally and physically fragile, I did not remember who had reached out.

We created a shrine by the window in her room, placing all her medals, prayer cards, figurines, candles, plaques, and cards of support, along with various spiritual and religious tokens that had been gifted to her on it. One of these things was the angel light, on a timer that would periodically light up. There was a necklace with Sierra's favorite symbol: God is Greater than the Highs and Lows.

There was Steven's family cross, a charm from Rome, and my father's cross from his funeral. We hung a collage of family pictures on the wall above it. Friends who own Robert Charles Photography in East Longmeadow, Massachusetts, had taken our family portraits and sent them all to us to add to the wall. And the flowers! Every day, bouquets of all sizes and varieties were delivered to her room from people we knew and did not know.

I was impressed by the people who showed up with so much love and grounded strength. Our close family friend and life coach, Lori, was one of these: steady and grounded, a pillar of strength for our family. There was absolutely no doubt in her mind that God would save Sierra, and she would be returned to us.

The folks at Steven's work also started reaching out; he had worked for The Home Depot for over twenty years and was well known and liked by his staff, as well as the corporate office. The love and outpouring of support from the employees of The Home Depot stores all over the country left us speechless; it was incredibly touching.

One of the first Home Depots to send us a picture of support from their employees had made a large sign that read #SierraStrong, which was quickly adopted by many, spreading throughout the stores, distribution centers, corporate offices, and board members. They all showed their support by wearing t-shirts and bracelets they had made, all reading #SierraStrong. Another store sent the angel lamp to sit by Sierra's bed, which became part of the shrine we made for her.

We had support from the friends we had made when we had lived in East Longmeadow, Massachusetts, for three years. People from our church, as well as friends and neighbors, all came together and started praying for Sierra and our family.

The day after the crash, Father Sam, the Catholic Chaplain, came to pray with us over Sierra's bed.

He brought a picture of the Divine Mercy - Jesus with His arms outstretched that said, "Jesus, I Trust in You."

He often came to pray with us, and a week or so later, when we taped the picture above the angel lamp, it lit up despite the timer not being set to turn on until that night. Our family members, who were supposed to be enjoying time with us in a fun way, were now with us, praying for Sierra's life instead. It was comforting having family around us, emotionally and spiritually, if it could not be physical.

We are very close with one of Steven's cousins (Carolyn) and her family, who live in New York State. We see them frequently as they return to Vermont a few times a year. Her two girls are close in age to Sierra and Aspen, and the girls always enjoy their cousin time. On the day of the crash, they had returned to New York state after visiting us all in Vermont for the July 4th long weekend and had been in close contact since hearing the news.

A week after the crash, they drove back to Vermont to visit us at Dartmouth. Lindsay had remained in close contact with them as they drove and organized Carolyn's Mom, Stepdad, and her brother to meet Steven's mom and dad, as well as Aspen, Tristan, and Tanner at Dartmouth. When I got the call that they were downstairs, I went down immediately. Even though they could not see Sierra, it was such a relief to see them and know that our family was there.

I have always believed that God shows us signs as indicators of his assistance in human affairs, and as we started to feel lifted by the unseen energy of all the prayers directed toward us, we became aware of signs everywhere, showing us that we were not alone.

It was just small things here and there at first; the neck brace supporting Sierra's head had the brand name Aspen printed across the front of it. We noticed the new boxes of gloves that had been restocked on the supply cart near Sierra's room now had the letters S, M, and L facing the front, spelling out Sierra's initials. When Aspen held her hand, she was sure she could feel very faint pressure, like Sierra was trying to squeeze her hand. Tristan would sit with her and sing her songs like they used to sing together when they would go fishing when she was younger. He also felt her gentle squeeze when he was holding her hand.

When Steven's parents drove to visit her every day in the hospital, her grandfather Steve would share with us the incredible rainbows he saw on the drive over. They stood out to him because he had not seen so many, so consistently, in all the years he had lived in the area. He was never really a church-going man, but he had started to pray again after hearing about the crash and asking God for a miracle.

The first brilliant rainbow he saw was right after he had asked for a sign. He would start to ask God where his rainbows were as he drove to and from the hospital every day, and almost every day, there were rainbows seen by not only him but all members of our family.

As we took turns dozing in the chair next to her bed, Steven and I would hear her voice whispering, "I'm okay."

The signs became more obvious, fueling my belief that with God's help, Sierra would return to us.

One night, I dreamt of tangled plants that had all fallen into each other in a pile, brown and dying, but as I untangled them, they grew upright and green again. I perceived that they were symbolic of Sierra's brain synapses and connections repairing themselves. I was sure it indicated Sierra would recover.

Two days after the crash, Aspen and her boyfriend were together in the pediatric intensive care family lounge. Aspen was crying, feeling futile and scared for her sister, and was praying. As they sat on the couch, her boyfriend stopped and asked Aspen if she was aware of a presence in the room.

He was sure there was an angel in the room with them. She did not feel it, but Aspen suddenly felt calm. A sense of reassurance came over her, and she stopped crying, more confident and hopeful that she would see Sierra wake up.

When Steven and I finally slept on Sunday night, we both dreamt of Sierra, and she told us she was OK. When Aspen slept, she too dreamed of Sierra; it was like she was communicating with us, letting us know she was still there.

One afternoon, I received a Facebook message from a complete stranger who'd heard about the crash through some acquaintances and felt compelled to reach out. She had just finished praying for Sierra and was randomly scrolling through YouTube when a particular video popped up, and she could not scroll past it. She shared a link to the YouTube video featuring St. Padre Pio, the patron saint of healing. Although our family is devout Catholics, I had never heard of St. Pio before the crash.

The video showed the story of how he had been instrumental in helping save a teenage girl the same age as Sierra, 25 years before. This wasn't the first time someone had mentioned this Saint, as his name had come up multiple times in conversations and messages from different people. This girl, Christine B., had also been in a life-altering crash, where she had teetered on the brink of death before a miracle brought her back. I felt connected to this family, and I immediately started praying to Saint Pio, too.

I went online to the National Center for Padre Pio and lit a virtual candle, as well as emailed the request asking for Sierra's healing. When I called the center later, they shared they had laid the intention at the feet of the statue of Saint Padre Pio. From that moment, I felt a warm presence to the left of me whenever I prayed to him.

I also looked up the family that had experienced the miracle of Padre Pio and called them, asking if they would pray for Sierra, too. The mother was so welcoming and supportive. I was touched by her compassion.

But Sierra wasn't making any progress; in fact, over the next few days, she was starting to get worse. We prayed harder.

By July 14th, things were looking bleak. Sierra had made no change, and they could not keep her in a medically induced coma for too much longer. The intention of an induced coma is to give the body and brain a break and to slow down the shock and the brain's response to massive trauma. The troubling thing was that she was on the highest doses of narcotics her body could handle, and her vitals were not improving.

She was fully dependent on machines to live, and it was just a matter of time before the doctors advised us to consider disconnecting the machines. The pressure on her brain was gradually mounting, and there was no room for it to expand. As a result, it was forcing more pressure into her brain stem, which was already severely injured.

To the medical professionals, it was only a matter of time before the swelling caused fatal damage to her already intensely injured brain. I did not want to understand; I was sure she wanted to return to us. They said they had exhausted all options; the only way to save her was to remove part of her skull to relieve the pressure, but it was not a viable surgery as her body was not strong enough to survive the operation.

They told us we needed to prepare for the next step and that we should call our priest to have her last rites given as she was not expected to live through the night. And on the slim chance she made it through the night, it would be a long road ahead, and there would not be much recovery due to the damage her brain had suffered. We would need to look at palliative care. They also told us if she did survive, we would be lucky if she would be able to sit up on her own or brush her teeth.

Understandably, this was devastating news. I could not speak and was overcome with emotion.

Steven stood up, took my hand, and announced in an authoritative manner, "We are done talking. You just do your job to the best of your ability, and we are going to leave the rest to God." We left the room.

Emotionally deflated and beyond desperate, I started the Facebook group "Miracle for Sierra – God's Heroes Unite" with the intention to garner more prayer warriors and post daily updates, letting people know of Sierra's progress and what was happening.

I felt it was my duty to let everyone know what was transpiring and to request more prayer warriors for our girl. I knew there would be people who would pray for our daughter. True heroes prevail in the direst of circumstances, and I felt, without a doubt, that people would send positive energy and blessings for a miracle.

This was my first post. This picture of Sierra hugging her dad was taken four days before the crash at a Fourth of July celebration. His smile emanated his happiness and joy, immersed in the connection they shared.

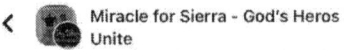

Miracle for Sierra - God's Heros Unite
Amy Jones Longmoore · Jul 14, 2020 · 🌐

I am sitting in the hospital room looking at my beautiful daughter as she lay in a coma. Her twin sister has not left her side. My husband and I are fatigued, but continue to feverishly pray. The prayers, support and energy from all of you is what is getting us through.

This week was our annual vacation in Maine, which we so much looked forward too, especially Sierra.

Monday was my father-in-law's birthday and tomorrow is my husband's birthday. Neither can celebrate, yet these are the two rocks that anchor our family during this incredibly hard time. Their wish is to have Sierra survive, come home and begin our journey to recovery.

A little later, we gathered around Sierra's bed as a family with Father Sam and prayed, reciting Psalm 23: The Lord Is My Shepherd. This psalm holds special significance in our family; Tristan, our eldest, even has it tattooed on his ribcage. As we spoke it over her, it took on an even deeper meaning for us. I was still a churning mess of emotions. I had been so sure she was going to make it. Surely God was not going to take her away now? I could not accept any other alternate ending besides the one where Sierra lives.

Early the next morning, I was praying in the hospital chapel. It was around 3 a.m., and I had left Steven in the room with Sierra. As I made my way to the chapel, the hospital was quiet, the chapel deserted. Instead of taking my usual seat, I knelt at the altar and asked in the name of God and the name of Jesus Christ for the miracle of bringing Sierra back to us.

I also asked for a sign that she would be returned to us. As I looked up past the altar and out the tall stained-glass window behind it into the darkness of the early morning, a bolt of lightning zig-zagged across the sky. I was so surprised I was transfixed, staring at the windowpane, but doubting the speed at which my request was affirmed, I asked for another sign.

When it happened again, I momentarily felt ashamed that I had doubted God. I was raised with and have retained a deep faith my entire life. It is a faith shared by my husband and entire family; I knew God would not desert us now.

The roller-coaster of uncertainty and worry was too much to bear. While I continued praying, I had a moment of surrender, where I accepted that God truly had the power to take her from us, just as he had given her to us in the first place. He had chosen us to be her parents, a wonderful gift to our family, with no time commitment. The only requirement was that we love her and raise her in faith.

As I understood this, I said aloud, "God, let your will be done."

At once, all the conflict I felt was eased, and I was at peace with God's plan, whatever that meant. The sense of peace that overtook me remained permanently from that moment; I was confident that whatever happened was part of His plan, even if it meant losing our little girl.

As I went back up to Sierra's room, I was aware of my mother's perfume, like she had just given me a hug and walked away. It was her signature scent, and I have never smelt it on anyone else since she passed away. I felt surrounded by love.

A little after that, early on the morning of July 15th, Dr. Perry Ball, the hospital's head neurosurgeon, was on duty in the Pediatric ICU. This was divine placement, as he was not usually assigned to the pediatric neuro unit. But as he reviewed Sierra's case, he realized she was not going to survive without the surgery to remove part of her skull and give her brain some room.

As the head neurosurgeon, he overrode the pediatric team's decision not to perform the risky surgery due to her condition, and he decided they needed to move ahead and fast. He was willing to do the operation that shift.

A different hospital Chaplain came in and introduced himself. He took Aspen, Steven, and me into another room, where we prayed before Dr. Ball came in and sat down with us to explain what he was going to do. Then he told us that she could die during the procedure. I understood that he had to tell us the huge risk, which was the reason they did not want to perform the surgery the previous day.

At around 4 a.m., with everything in place, Dr Ball and his neurosurgery team burst into the room and said, "We are taking Sierra down for surgery now."

We were surprised, thinking they would be operating in a few hours, but the team was also concerned for Sierra's prognosis, knowing that she physically may not be able to cope with the surgery.

With every passing minute, her brain continued to swell, and without the surgery, her prospect of survival was almost zero. We followed her inanimate body on the gurney all the way to the operating room, kissing her and telling her we loved her and would be right there waiting for her when she was done.

We sat in anticipation, not knowing if she would survive the surgery. We headed back to her room and waited. We fervently prayed for her survival. Her life was in God's hands.

Dr. Ball was able to perform the radical surgery in only an hour and a half with textbook success. He and his team removed the entire front part of Sierra's skull and placed sensors on her brain along with a thick layer of mesh under her skin to protect her brain from where the part of her skull was missing. This allowed her brain enough room to swell, and within hours, the pressure on her brain had diminished and was under control. I knew he had been sent from God at the exact time he was needed most. This was the miracle we prayed for. This surgery had saved her life!

Amid our exhaustion and heartfelt pain, we somehow managed to feel energized, inspired, and hopeful that Sierra would now have a chance to survive. We were uplifted as we saw her gurney coming down the hallway and being wheeled back into her room. Many doctors and nurses were trailing beside and behind her to ensure she was once again properly connected to all her monitors and lifesaving supports.

It was Steven's birthday, and he was humbled that he could not have wished for a better birthday present. Although not entirely in the clear, she remained heavily sedated and fully dependent on the ventilator. Her body was still unable to regulate her temperature, at times requiring an arctic blanket to bring down her dangerously high fevers. It was decided that it was time to start weaning her off the paralytic medication, keeping her in a coma.

Still, we prayed, keeping vigil at her bedside. Father Sam came regularly and prayed with us as well. A friend who is a Reiki practitioner came and did Reiki over her. Her high school had "Sierra Strong" on their electronic sign at the entrance for weeks while regularly posting updates to the community. Family members who could not be at her bedside got together with her grandparents and created a healing garden under a tree on their land that she and Aspen liked to visit frequently when they were younger.

The #SierraStrong movement took off quickly. Her school guidance department reached out to let us know the school and community were raising funds for our immediate family, who needed gas to travel to and from the hospital and food while we were absent.

Lindsay was also fundraising and organizing bracelets and T-shirts to be distributed and sold. She had contacts at many local businesses and stores and would meet people in public places (because of the COVID restrictions) and get them boxes of bracelets and T-shirts.

I continued to post daily updates about Sierra's progress on the "Miracle for Sierra-God's Heroes Unite" Facebook page that was growing quite a prayer group following. We had messages from all over the U.S.A. and the world, people who had experienced similar situations sharing their stories, offering hope, and letting us know they were there and praying for her recovery.

People shared their stories of feeling drawn to pray for Sierra and our family, even though many of them had not been to church for years. Often, I would be crying tears of gratitude and joy as I read the messages and emails at the outpouring of love directed toward us. People rediscovered their faith as they joined together in prayer for Sierra; I felt God's love through it all.

Her prognosis was slightly less grim; we were told she would probably remain in a vegetative state along with a host of other afflictions, but we were beyond grateful she was alive. Every morning, the medical team would come in and perform tests on her, checking her brain response and eye dilation. It was predicted she would be blind in her left eye, and if we were lucky, she would eventually be able to learn how to do some simple tasks for herself, but she would never be fully independent and would always need a caring person in her life.

We were given a prayer blanket by one of Sierra's friends who had survived childhood cancer. The blanket was made by a local mom whose son had also sustained a traumatic brain injury. He had so much internal damage, broken bones, and trauma to his brain that they did not predict that he would survive. His mom stayed in the hospital with him for 28 days, not wanting to leave her child until she knew he would recover.

During that time, she crocheted the prayer blanket, embedding each row with love and prayers for healing as she sat in her son's room. Once her son had healed enough to return home, the blanket was passed on to another family whose teen had been seriously injured in a crash and sustained a TBI. This mom offered us guidance and advice for the journey ahead, noting that navigating the healing of the brain was by far the most difficult part of the journey. She offered her time and advice if we needed it, particularly as we moved into the next phase of Sierra's recovery.

The blanket was then passed on to Sierra's friend while she was going through cancer treatment, and then it came to us. It was beautiful, very light and warm, and incredibly special; you could sense the loving, healing energy it radiated. This blanket stayed by Sierra's side throughout her journey.

After the pressure had been controlled in her brain, they started weaning her off the medication that was keeping her in a deep, comatose state. They began a very slow 10-day withdrawal period to bring her off the powerful drugs that had kept her brain quiet to give her body and brain a chance to rest and heal.

Steven's cousin Carolyn and her family came back to support us. Before they came, Carolyn had gone to her local Catholic Gift Shop in New York to buy a few things for us and Sierra. The store owner gave her a gift to give to Steven and me, which was a St Padre Pio prayer pamphlet. This stood out as another powerful sign that he was close by and looking out for our family.

We also started using Doterra essential oils and used a diffuser in her room to stimulate the olfactory parts of her brain. Knowing how powerful the smell is, we wanted to try every viable option available to us to help stimulate and heal her brain.

Her medical team assured us at this point that with her intracranial pressure reduced, she had turned the corner. Even though she was still reliant on a ventilation system to assist with her breathing and a feeding tube for nutrition, we were confident she would start the healing process. This was great news! Replaying in our minds what we had been told by Dr. Dan about "just fighting for survival" now seemed like a distant memory.

Although progress in her condition was in barely measurable steps, they were still stepping forward. She still faced challenges where things would seem to go backward, though. But we did not lose faith. We prayed to St. Padre Pio and God, grateful for the journey so far and their intervention.

By July 22nd, Sierra was starting to develop pneumonia from being intubated and attached to a ventilator for so long. Just seven days prior, Sierra had undergone major surgery to have part of her skull removed, and now she was going back under anesthesia for another surgery. With any surgery, there are risks, and this was no different.

I remember my husband and I signing the waiver outlining all the risks, including death. Here, we were on a positive trajectory, knowing she was going to survive while signing another waiver with the understanding that she may not. The feelings of contrast bubbled up inside, and the fear of what could happen was real. We handed our anguish and fears over to God. He was steering the course of her journey.

The surgeon and otolaryngologist successfully performed a tracheotomy, where a tube is surgically placed in the windpipe at the front of the neck to assist with breathing. It would deliver humidified oxygen to help her breathe on her own again. Five days later, they weaned her to a CPAP machine and placed a tracheostomy collar, which is a soft plastic mask that fits over and around the tracheostomy tube. It was another important step towards easing her dependence on the machines that were so integral to her survival.

> "Pray, hope, and don't worry
>
> Prayer is the key to God's heart."
>
> St Padre Pio

Chapter Four – Sierra at Spaulding

[28] Come to Me, all *you* who labor and are heavy laden, and I will give you rest. Matthew 11:28

"A miracle is a surprising and welcome event that is not explicable by natural or scientific laws. A miracle is what everyone prays for when all hope is lost".

A person waking up from a coma is not like the way it is portrayed in movies and on TV, where someone just kind of wakes up from a big sleep, but it is more of a process. Sierra started having serious withdrawals from the powerful barbiturates that had been used to keep her unconscious for almost two weeks. Her body started neurostorming, which is when there is a sudden and exaggerated stress response because of the damage sustained to the brain.

It is the brain's "fight-or-flight" response, which had been put on hold due to the powerful drugs that kept her unconscious. As the brain takes back control, it triggers spikes in temperature along with elevated blood pressure and brain activity, rapid breathing and a racing heartbeat, stiff arms and legs, and restlessness.

She had a helmet to protect her head, where they had removed the section of her skull, and her heart rate and blood pressure were continually monitored as well. Her arms had to be restrained to stop her from ripping off her dressings in moments of intense agitation. These moments would be fleeting but scary. Mostly, she was barely conscious. When she was technically "awake," she was minimally aware of her surroundings.

Her brain was slowly coming back into operation and was desperately reacting to the trauma that occurred almost three weeks before. Due to the severity of her brain injury, this confused state of consciousness could last for weeks.

The medical team continued with their daily performance checks on Sierra; they would shout and clap and prod her, looking for a response. We were seeing some early responsiveness, small indicators like her right pupil dilating in response to bright light, and some involuntary movement to sound and touch. She was starting to open her eyes but very minimally. They still asserted that she would likely be blind in her left eye.

There was talk of the next steps for her, that she was to be transferred to a rehabilitation hospital and she would receive daily physical and mental rehabilitation. Again, we were told that with some good rehabilitation, one day, she could possibly sit up unassisted and perhaps brush her teeth on her own. They weren't very encouraging.

From the very beginning, an acquaintance I worked with years ago reached out selflessly due to her own experience with brain injury; her son had been in a terrible car crash seven years before. She was so kind and helpful throughout; I was grateful for her thoughts. She was adamant we have Sierra transferred to the

Spaulding Rehabilitation Hospital in Boston, which is one of the best pediatric rehabilitation centers in the world, and she would receive the best care and rehabilitation there.

Our medical team was trying to get her placed at Franciscan Hospital outside of Boston. We were told Sierra wasn't a candidate for Spaulding as she was vegetative and still had a trach in place, but at the insistence of this kindhearted woman, we pushed continually for her to be transferred there.

I was taught how to feed her through a tube in her stomach, change and bathe her, as I would become her constant care person. We were encouraged by the continual small gains we saw; she started to show small movements, and her vitals stabilized. It was decided she should be moved to the PICU step-down unit, although her doctors were unsure of the best place for her because she was still largely unresponsive.

I continued to post daily updates on the "Miracle for Sierra – God's Heroes Unite" Facebook page, where I would note how many days had passed since the crash and what we had experienced that day. Even her smallest accomplishments were celebrated and recognized, and we continued to pray.

Our Reiki practitioner friend had taken a photo with her and continued to do Reiki therapy remotely, and another lady would call regularly to play the harp for her on speakerphone. We played instrumental music specifically for TBI to stimulate her brain response. We continued to surround her with prayer and positivity, thankful for her life and the devoted nurses and doctors who worked with her.

Miracle for Sierra – God's Heros Unite (Facebook post)

August 2, 2020

Day 25: "Stay with me, Lord, because I am weak, and I need your strength, that I may not fall so often." ~ St. Padre Pio

Every moment feels like an eternity when your child is severely injured. You feel helpless, empty, and confused; dark days are frequent. But then there is hope, faith, family, friends, community, and support from those you don't even know. God governs those interactions and provides the outreach needed to see us through.

Sierra is in her new room, which is an instance in life when "downgrading "is a win. Vitals are stable. The ventilator is gone. She is healing. Miraculously, she is healing and showing signs of strength and repair. Again, there are too many unknowns until she becomes more responsive.

"Where our strength runs out, God's strength begins."

We were continually lifted by the unceasing prayer messages and flowers and gifts people sent. We still receive many kind thoughts, prayers, and messages of support every day. We knew that this was God guiding them and giving us the strength and hope needed for Sierra's journey.

One day, when Steven and I were sitting with her, she made facial expressions of a huge smile followed by extreme sorrow and dismay. It was like she was trying to cry. This was heartbreaking, to say the least. The medical team dismissed these expressions as involuntary movements caused by a reflex response. Steven was terrified at the thought that Sierra might be trapped in her body forever. We felt helpless and empty.

We knew she was still in there, fighting the restrictions of her body and brain, desperately trying to heal and communicate with us. Her eyes were open a lot more, and although she had an unfocused, blank stare, we would still show her things people had sent and read the cards and messages to her. Letting her know we were always there with her was important to us.

One morning, it was decided that fresh air would be good for her. It took a lot of planning and coordination to move her limp body from her hospital bed to a medical wheelchair to wheel her outside. They used a lanyard and pulley system to hoist her in and out of bed. It was a beautiful sunny day when we got her outside, but we could tell she did not recognize her change of surroundings even though her eyes were open.

She was surrounded by people who loved her: me, Steven, his dad, Aspen, several nurses, and a respiratory therapist. She couldn't hold her head up, had no control of her body, and was unaware of her surroundings. At the time, I hoped it might trigger something in her subconscious, but I later realized they probably did that for our benefit more than Sierra's.

That was the first time Steven and I had stepped out of the hospital since July 8th. It was now August 5th.

The outpouring of love and support continued to flow as family and friends posted pictures of themselves on social media wearing their #Sierrastrong shirts and praying for her to progress.

Sierra peacefully lay in her bed with Aspen's favorite stuffed animal nestled under her arm. The tattered Siberian Husky deemed "Wolfy" had been through the wash countless times. Aspen was given this priceless treasure when she was just a few days old in the NICU. We draped his neck with sentimental rosaries and medals, and he became Sierra's protector. She was never without him throughout this whole journey.

August 7th was the day Aspen had her senior portraits taken. I clearly remember that morning. She fretted because this was another event she and Sierra had planned to do together. How could she smile and pretend to be happy for her upcoming senior year without her twin sister by her side? Aspen decided to take one of the lawn signs with her that showed three pictures of Sierra with a caption that read #Sierrastrong. She found a significant way to include Sierra in her portraits.

The next day, we were still pushing for Sierra to be transferred to Spaulding. Her condition was stagnating, and there were many conversations between the medical staff, us, and Spaulding about her transfer. We prayed so fervently for God to direct the decision. As I sat in Sierra's room, deep in thought and prayer, I looked out the window, and there was a beautiful, bright rainbow hovering over the hospital. Not soon thereafter, much to our surprise, it was eventually decided she would be transferred to Spaulding.

<u>Miracle for Sierra – God's Heros Unite (Facebook Post)</u>

August 11, 2020

Day 34: "You are uniquely you. It is okay for you to be who you are. It is certainly okay for you to be yourself. A living, breathing human being with feelings." ~ Lynne Namka

As we updated last night, today, we travel to our next step. Boston, here we come for Rehab. Last night was exciting as Sierra cried, laughed, and smiled for the first time. Amy and I were so amazed and emotional with her. God has great things to come. #SierraStrong

"Man says, show me, and I will trust you. God says, trust me, and I will show you." Psalm 126:6

On August 11, 2020, Sierra was transferred to Spaulding Rehabilitation. It was noted that she had emerged from a minimally conscious state and was experiencing post-traumatic amnesia, which is a state of confusion or memory loss that occurs immediately following a traumatic brain injury. She was unable to sit or walk independently when she was admitted.

Spaulding only has one pediatric floor with twelve beds, and it is a secure facility that had extra measures in place because of COVID. It didn't take long for us to settle her into her room. The 8th floor had an incredible sweeping view of Boston Harbor below.

Steven and I stayed with her, and we met with her assigned care team of doctors, and they outlined the treatment plan for her. Based on the information they received from Dartmouth and what they observed themselves, they were minimally optimistic about her recovery. She needed moderate to maximum verbal cues for attention.

She was unable to speak and had difficulty expressing her needs and understanding verbal information. They estimated that she would be there for at least two months, but her stay could extend beyond Christmas. By this time, however, Steven and I knew that God had his own plan for her, and we quietly continued praying for a full recovery, asking for prayers for a full recovery, too. It's all we wanted.

Her bed was encased with a giant secure mesh tent for her own safety, and each night, she was barricaded in by pillows and padding. She was still hooked up to all sorts of machines, not being able to eat or drink or even breathe on her own yet. The routine every night consisted of having elbow compression sleeves fitted and her arms and wrists restrained to keep her from pulling out her trach tube.

She also had to wear giant medical mittens, eye lubricant, and eye patches, and her trach tube would be cleaned, numerous medications administered, and special wound care for her head, which was still healing from her skull surgery. It was intimidating and extremely involved, with the whole process taking almost an hour.

Sierra was placed on a five-day therapy schedule, and there was little change in the first two weeks. She looked like a rag doll in therapy as they moved her lifeless arms and legs around. She had no control over her head or her body. Her team did not give up; they were all incredibly positive and enthusiastic, which was heartwarming.

Still, I posted updates on the Facebook page. I was encouraged by our interactions with so many caring people. We prayed multiple times a day, thanking Padre Pio for holding her up and for God to watch over Sierra's medical and therapy teams so that their work would positively impact her brain and that it would heal.

Our community was more supportive than ever. Local newspapers were still following her story, and #SierraStrong signs were showing up all over the Newbury and Bradford areas and beyond. We felt a massive groundswell of continued support.

Sierra's ex, however, was apparently still obsessed with finding out what she remembered. He had attempted to enter Spaulding Hospital twice, confidently walking straight through security without a mask or invitation. He had also discovered her room number and started calling incessantly.

Feeling that his actions had crossed the line, which we did not have the time, energy, or inclination to indulge in, we disconnected the phone and had her admission documents changed to an alias. We decided to let whatever it was on this boy's heart be between him and God.

However, just because our family had no interest in his desperate actions for attention, it did not mean that he stopped. He and his friends started turning up at our house at all hours of the day and night, demanding attention. He became such a nuisance that we had security cameras installed, and on August 21st, we filed a No Trespass order with the State of Vermont. He made hundreds of calls to Sierra's phone and family members' phones.

Steven and I had also discovered all of Sierra's phone and text message history from this boy. We were stunned. Along with the No Trespass order, near the end of August, I also submitted a Relief from Abuse Order against him on Sierra's behalf.

Her phone history revealed that on the morning of the crash, a couple of days after she broke up with him, she had a 26-minute phone call with him. There were multiple text messages from him, at first pleading and begging, and then when she didn't respond the way he wanted her to, he became threatening and intimidating.

Suddenly, things felt a lot more sinister, and his constant pushing for information about what Sierra remembered took on a new, disturbing slant. We had Steven's family stay at the house with Tristian, Lindsay, and Tanner, and still, he continued, with him and his friends parking on our road and riding their dirt bikes up and down the road past our house for hours at a time, revving their motors.

Despite his desperation for attention, we continued to focus on Sierra. Sierra's PT team introduced a tilt table to help her regain vertical weight distribution because she had laid flat for so long, and her muscles had atrophied.

The first day was difficult; they barely raised her body strapped to the table like a rag doll, and she had to lay her back down again due to the massive stress response she had to the change in gravity on her body. I remember thinking if getting her this far took three weeks, how on earth would we be going home in eight weeks?

We started to focus our prayers on the next step she needed to take in the healing process, and right then, it was conquering the tilt table. Our prayer warriors came together, and we prayed for her success with the tilt table. It took three weeks for her to be able to attain a fully vertical upright position without her blood pressure skyrocketing and heart rate becoming extremely erratic. But she did it, and we celebrated.

It was positive progress. And one of many small steps that we started seeing every day.

Steven and I made the decision for each of us to take turns returning home; one would stay with Sierra for the week, and the other would return home to be with our other children. The Home Depot had been incredible to us and Steven throughout all of this; their support had certainly eased the stress of the situation. Neither of us had been home for almost six weeks.

During that time, our youngest, Tanner, had hit his growth spurt and shot up four inches, as well as all the other changes that go along with a growing teenage boy. It broke my heart that his mom and dad had not been there for him.

At least with one or the other of us there, it would countercheck some of the parental absences for them. They had supported each other so well and had their grandparents with other family members stepping in, too, but it's not the same when mom and dad are not home.

Hardly seeing Steven, however, was very difficult. We leaned on each other heavily up until that point, and being separated was mentally and emotionally tough. We talked dozens of times a day, but I had not realized up until then how much strength I had gained from a glance or an encouraging look from him. I missed him tremendously.

Sierra's room had a big picture window and an incredible view, overlooking the beautiful Boston harbor and the boardwalk at the edge. I would sit at the window in Sierra's room while she was still sleeping, surrounded by her favorite soft toys from when she was much younger, and imagine one day being able to walk the boardwalk with Sierra and Aspen together, laughing and talking.

I felt sad and hopeless; the reality of the severity of brain injuries and seeing the kids check out of the pediatric ward only marginally better than when they came in was disheartening. I wanted so much more for Sierra.

Around August 19, I was once again deep in prayer and found myself asking God for another sign, specifically a triple rainbow. I didn't even know if that was a thing, and momentarily felt bad that God would take it as a challenge by a person of little faith, but I knew that both Steven and I (and most likely other family members too) had bargained with God, offering ourselves in exchange for Sierra. I needed reassurance.

After about two weeks of Sierra remaining unresponsive, she started tracking objects with her eyes and was gaining small independent movements of her head.

It was August 24th, and Steven was sitting in the rocking chair looking at Sierra, feeling immense sadness that he hadn't heard her voice in 47 days. He prayed to God for the opportunity to hear her voice at least one more time.

He had no idea that God was about to grant him his wish. Moments later, while he was kneeling by her bedside, he held her hand, made eye contact with Sierra, and told her he loved her very much.

At that moment, she mouths out the words, "I love you."

He was shocked! He was so floored that he fell further on his knees to the ground and, with excitement, hit the nurse's button and asked them to come witness what he just heard Sierra say. He then asked Sierra to say it again so he could send a video home to the family.

Sierra, in a very raspy voice, uttered "I love you" to Steven.

The nurses were so excited and happy to reassure Steven this was a huge step forward! He was elated! At that point, Steven was convinced Sierra would not only recover but would walk out of Spaulding on her own with no assistance, feeding tubes, or trach.

I was kneeling next to our bed at home with my kids around me when Steven called and sent us the video of her saying I love you.

We broke down and cried as we could not imagine when we would hear our baby girl's voice again.

Speaking was extremely hard for her. She would get upset and frustrated that she could not form the words, and it was especially difficult with the trach tube in place.

As the words "I love you" were verbalized strongly and used more frequently by Sierra, the next words she said were, "He hit me."

Steven was confused; she was hard to understand and barely coherent, but he was so overjoyed that Sierra was able to communicate he did not return to it until some time later.

Five days a week, she was taken to physical therapy, and her body and head moved around to reintroduce some muscle tone as well as a range of movement. She was extremely fortunate that her body had remained unscathed in the crash, but she still had little control over it.

Around August 25th, we felt encouraged; she was beginning to move her head, just a little on her own, holding it up for short periods of time by herself. Little by little, she was getting stronger and more alert; her eye movements were more controlled for longer periods of time, and she was becoming more responsive.

The continued support from all sorts of people reaching out to us throughout her stay in Spaulding was frequent and such a boost, from the gifts that were sent to the visitors from Home Depot who showed up outside with placards and balloons to let us know they were sending all their positive vibes. God was putting us in these people's hearts at the perfect time to buoy our flagging spirits and lift our hopes. It forever changed the way I think about how one person can make such a positive difference in someone else's life.

Every day, I would journal the day's progress on the "Miracle for Sierra" Facebook page. I would quote a prayer or an inspiration of some sort, and then I would add updates on her progress and close with another prayer and #SierraStrong, plus a picture. I felt it was my duty to keep everyone aware of her progress. I did not want anyone to forget her. She still had so far to go. It became a valued ritual for me as well.

Amy Jones Longmoore

August 24, 2020 ·

Day 47: "Where you are today is no accident. God is using this situation you are in right now to shape you and prepare you for the place He wants to bring you into tomorrow. Trust Him with His plan even if you don't understand it."

Sierra spent time outside yesterday. The weather was beautiful. First full day off for her since she arrived. She laughed a lot with her twin sister Aspen, who spent the weekend visiting. Gearing up for a busy Monday, though. Lots to accomplish this week. We are so blessed by the grace of God. ♥🙏 #SierraStrong

"God doesn't give you the people you want in your life. He gives you the people you need in your life. To help you, to hurt you, to love you, to leave you, and to make you the person you were meant to be."

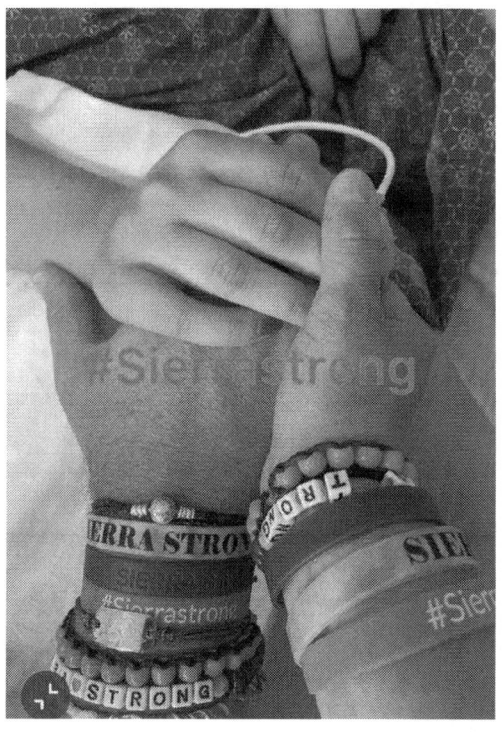

At last, Sierra was able to sit up, assisted with stabilized vitals, and almost immediately began intensive therapies on machines to get her muscles moving again. Time passed agonizingly slowly during those first few weeks at Spaulding. The seconds seemed like minutes, the minutes felt like hours, and the hours felt like an eternity.

Due to the COVID restrictions, we were limited to the eighth floor, and the only way we could get Sierra out of her room for a change of scenery was to walk laps with Sierra, pushing her around the hallways of the twelve-room ward. It took a lot of time to get Sierra out of bed and into the wheelchair.

Steven and I, along with the help of several staff members, connected her to a lanyard, got her situated in the chair, strapped her in, restrained her wrists, and padded around her head with several pillows to stabilize it. We made sure that each ordeal of getting her out of bed was worth it by walking hours around and around the eighth floor. We walked countless miles pushing her around that ward.

Still, people we did not know were reaching out to us, letting us know we were not alone. We heard from a British champion cross-channel swimmer who was an amputee, a lovely man who sent Sierra an autographed shirt and one of his medals, along with the reassurance that he would pray for her. The continued support was encouraging and uplifting when things felt too overwhelming. It was touching to know people were praying for Sierra and our family.

And the gifts! People sent all sorts of pampering and spa gifts to Spaulding for Sierra so that we could spoil her. There were diffusers and special healing blends of Doterra oils, along with the oils we had been using for a month or so. Color Street nails and all sorts of other luxurious lotions, masks, and creams. One afternoon, we had a "spa session," and Sierra lay still long enough for me to put the nails on her.

They looked lovely for the afternoon, but because she was so restless, she bit them all off by the next day. She had extraordinarily little control over her impulses to scratch at herself and had to be in wrist restraints a lot of the time so that she did not pull out her trach or scratch at the dressing on her head where she was still missing the piece of skull they had removed.

Sierra was so sweet and loving as she was becoming more self-aware. Apparently, this is rare when recovering from a TBI. We had been warned that there was a good chance she would be angry and confused, but Sierra was not. She was an absolute sweetheart to everyone.

One gloomy, rainy day, as I was sitting in Sierra's room, I read while she slept. I was aware that the room seemed brighter. I looked up from my book; the sky was lighter outside, the clouds clearing above us and over Boston Harbor, and as I took in what I was seeing, I was amazed. Right there in front of me, as I had requested, three rainbows.

Two in the sky and one perfectly reflected in the water. I could see three distinct rainbows. The sign I had asked for was right in front of me. I was filled with a sense of peace and comfort. God was still in control. He taught us many lessons along the way. He would take care of everything, and our faith in Him would be with us on the long road ahead.

Learning how to control her head and sitting up by herself were major accomplishments that took weeks for her to master through the rigorous PT she was doing five days a week. Movement on the right side of her body was gradually coming back, but her left side was almost paralyzed because of the midbrain stroke she had experienced in the crash.

On August 28th, PT started her on the movement machines to get her muscles working and strengthened for everyday activities. There was a walking machine that she was strapped to, and her legs and feet were moved in the motion of walking. It was fascinating to me that they could safely simulate the physical action of her walking to strengthen those muscles and trigger muscle memory, even if she was physically incapable of doing it herself.

Occupational Therapy worked with her on eye tracking, convergence, peripheral vision (she had none of these when she started OT), and awareness of sound and light. Sierra was not responding well to those tests. Holding onto things like a foam ball was also not available to her. She had little control of her hands or finger strength.

Having her tracheostomy tube capped as the last step before it was removed and she could breathe on her own again was a long and awful process. I did not realize until then that she would have to learn the muscle memory of how to breathe again. They would cap it, and she couldn't breathe, or she would start choking and coughing, so they'd have to leave the cap off. Watching her gasp for air made us feel even more helpless than we had already felt.

It was as if our breath had stopped as our hearts sank back into our chests, not allowing our lungs to fill with air. They tried multiple times a week for almost two weeks before they could cap it for a 24-hour period, then they gradually increased the amount of time it was capped until finally they capped it for good, and she could begin speech therapy. It was decided to keep the tube in place until she had mastered breathing on her own for a significant amount of time.

Her therapists spent a lot of time focusing on what she could remember in speech and language, drawing it out of her, teaching her how to form words and where her tongue placement should be. They also started introducing liquified solids and thickened liquids as she learned how to swallow all over again.

These were small steps, but the impact was significant.

One week, when I got back to Spaulding after my week at home, Steven met me in the hall. I asked him what he was doing there. He said the OT therapist was in there, and the doctor had asked him to wait outside. So here he was.

As we stood there speculating what could be happening, the doctor ran out flustered, excitedly declaring, "Sierra is reading! I can't believe she is reading! Come and see!"

We rushed into the room, and Sierra was reading out loud!

Her milestones would sneak up on us like that; we often felt like she had reached the point where she would go no further, but then she would surprise us with a massive leap forward.

Steven was her most influential coach; he is such an amazing man of God and loves his family with such devotion. Everything he does is with intention and purpose, and he loves his children with all his heart, especially his hunting partner. He was always there to encourage her and remind her how talented and capable she was. Her dad was her biggest motivator, too.

When she was struggling while relearning how to kick a soccer ball and regain movement in her legs, she became disheartened and wanted to give up, but he immediately stepped in to remind her how she used to walk our German shepherd, Brooklyn, and how Brooklyn always went to her when it was time to go out. This was very motivating for her, and she instantly perked up and regained her energy to keep trying. Even though she was exhausted, she started moving her legs and kicked the soccer ball.

Steven figured out the most effective way to keep her motivated was to remind her of what she used to be able to do and how capable she was. As Sierra progressed physically, all members of our extended family continued seeing rainbows everywhere. It was a season of rainbows. Every time someone came to visit Sierra or left the hospital, there was guaranteed to be a big, bright, beautiful rainbow in the sky, even over our house.

As Sierra came back to us and grew stronger, the doctors had warned us (and shown us on CAT scans) that the parts of Sierra's brain that governed her personality had been severely damaged and that she would not be the same person she was before the crash. We did not know what to expect. Medical staff had warned us on multiple occasions while she was still in a coma that TBI patients were angry and ornery as they recovered.

Sierra had been very introverted before the crash, so we presumed she held back and was just taking it all in as she would have previously. She had no problem remembering family members, and she was able to recognize her therapists, but it was a little more difficult for her to remember her nurses, as they rotated regularly.

To our surprise, her demeanor remained very sweet and loving, often repeating phrases like "I'm sorry" when we would do things for her.

Sierra's skull replacement was to be an important milestone in her therapy. We were told by several members of her medical team that once that was back in place, it was normal for children to experience significant progress in their rehabilitation.

This was promising. She had really turned the corner and was making some definite progress, being able to read and move her body at will, but the thought of something able to assist in making that happen faster was very exciting for us all.

The surgery was scheduled for September 4, 2020. She would be taken by ambulance back to Dartmouth Hitchcock for the operation. We could not wait.

Six days before the scheduled surgery, a nursing assistant was taking care of Sierra's daily bathing by herself, which was a task that normally took two people, as she was still so restless when unrestrained, and it was important to control her hands. In a flash, Sierra scratched and grabbed at her head, tearing off all the scabs from her first surgery and opening the wound.

We were genuinely concerned, knowing that her replacement surgery was in less than a week. The wound care team at Spaulding assured us that they could have it closed and healed enough with the use of medical-grade nutrition for the surgery to proceed. The day arrived, and we took the 2.5-hour ambulance ride to Dartmouth Hitchcock Hospital and waited all day for the surgery to happen.

Dr. Ball finally came in to greet us; he inspected her wound and turned to us, looking very grim. He told us he could not perform the surgery that day due to exposure to bacteria that could potentially get under the skin and infect the skull that was being replaced.

He had no choice but to cancel the operation. As a double blow, the whole front piece of her skull that had been frozen for preservation had been defrosting all day, and they were not sure if it would be viable for refreezing and replacement.

They also could not give us a date right then that the operation could be performed. The anticipation of a positive change that we had waited and prepared for was struck down at the last minute. I could hold it together no longer and fell to the floor sobbing.

I could not believe this was happening. Steven and I were thoroughly deflated and demoralized. Steven wondered how he would find the energy to stay awake to protect the front of her head where her skull was missing, as he had done for 52 days now.

The ambulance drove us back to Spaulding in silence, and we took Sierra back up to her room. She had not had any nutrition or hydration for 24 hours at this point, in anticipation of the surgery, so they fed her nearly twice the regular amount through the feeding tube. I had recommended a couple of smaller feedings, but my recommendation was not listened to. I did not push it because I was drained and just did not have the energy.

After a full feed to compensate for her lack of nutrition, Sierra was organized for the night's rest. Right after everyone left the room, she started vomiting, and because she could not sit up or turn her head, she started choking on her vomit. She was locked in this zippered medical mesh tent, and we could not get to her. It was beyond horrifying! Here was our daughter, choking to death right in front of us, and we could not get into the mesh tent that surrounded her to help her.

As the nurses and doctors were running into the room to help her, I left my body, incredulous that after everything we had been through, I was going to watch her choke to death in front of me. NOW? I have never felt so helpless, demoralized, and low. I could not understand God's plan at that point. It felt like he had forgotten us.

We had reached the bottom. Steven and I were exhausted physically, drained emotionally, and destroyed mentally. I did not have any tears left to cry by this point. It felt like a dark cloud had descended upon us.

Utterly defeated, we prayed together that night for another sign, as we knew our faith was being tested once again.

Chapter Five – Tides Turn

> 2 The LORD protects and preserves them—
> they are counted among the blessed in the land—
> he does not give them over to the desire of their foes.
> 3 The LORD sustains them on their sickbed
> and restores them from their bed of illness. Psalm 41:2-3

Following Sierra's operation being postponed and her nearly choking to death on her own vomit, she was cleaned up and changed, along with her bedding and dressings. She had a good night's rest. Her PT appointment the next day was early. Still feeling discouraged, I did my best to put on a happy face. It was a new day. If God did not have a bigger plan for Sierra, we would not still be here, right? I kept reminding myself that He was in control.

Sierra had a new therapist that morning. She introduced herself as Jen and was very upbeat and positive. She told us she would be pushing Sierra's limits that day. Steven and I nodded and smiled politely. Feeling demoralized from yesterday's events, I vaguely wondered if she had read Sierra's case notes.

As the session progressed, the therapist asked Steven to hold the wheelchair as she helped Sierra up and told Sierra that this was the day she was going to walk. Steven and I just looked at each other, not knowing what to expect.

Much to our delight and surprise, Sierra was able to support her own weight, and then she took six steps holding on to her therapist. Steven had rolled the wheelchair up behind her, and she took a rest and then stood up and did it again! Twelve steps gave us all the faith we needed.

Steven and I cried tears of joy, knowing that God had given us His sign. True to Sierra's way, and with God's assistance, she would do this at her own pace, which was perfect.

Amy Jones Longmoore

September 6, 2020

Day 61: "God doesn't give us what we can handle. God helps us handle what we are given."

Sierra's surgeries were postponed. After a long day of travel, she is back, working on her recovery. Much to our amazement, she took her first steps with assistance. She is fierce, strong-willed, and determined. Thank you, God, for entrusting us to be her parents. We thank you for keeping Sierra in your prayers as you give thanks to God this Sunday. God Bless all our heroes.#Sierrastrong

"God always gives His best to those who leave the choice with Him." ~ Psalm 37:7

After those first steps, there was no stopping her. Within a few days, she was independently walking with a walker. By September 12, just one week after her first assisted steps, she had graduated from the walker and was walking at a steady pace while supported from behind by her PT therapists. She practiced walking while attached to a harness several times a day.

Over the next month, as her therapies progressed, she got stronger and stronger. Our fierce-spirited girl was coming back in small but significant moments, and she was determined. With Steven coaching her through her harness sessions, she was quickly ready to climb stairs.

We continually kept her alert and curious by playing "brain" music, singing songs, dancing around her room, reading books with her, and watching her favorite movies on her iPad. We continued to diffuse Doterra essential oils daily to stimulate her olfactory regions of the brain, and we used targeted oil blends to provide emotional support as well.

We got to experience Sierra growing up all over again, going from being completely dependent on everyone around her like a newborn to learning how to control her body, hold herself up, experience food, and learn how to hold a spoon and feed herself. She was also learning how to walk, talk, read, and more. We were watching her re-learn her life stages. It was every bit as exciting as it had been when she went through it all the first time.

But it could also be heartbreaking as she re-experienced all her painful memories again. One day, she asked where her grandmother (my mother) was, who had passed away five years before. Another time, she wanted to know how one of our deceased family pets was doing. Steven and I would compare notes and discuss which parts of her life she was re-living; it was gut-wrenching at times. Do we tell her the truth and upset her? Or lie to spare her feelings?

We knew we could not lie to her, but watching her process this type of news as if she had never heard it before was awful. No matter how gently we broke it to her, we all would end up in tears. This would also happen with her joyful moments too. Seeing her realize and remember things she could do, or songs she liked, or reliving happy memories was every bit as heartwarming as the grief had been heartbreaking.

And sometimes, the surprises of her recovered memories were encouraging. One day, when Aspen was hanging out with Sierra, she asked her to braid her hair the way she used to; Aspen had always loved it when Sierra did her hair. And Sierra just did it without a thought. This was no mean feat, as Aspen's hair was very long, almost down to her waist. We were becoming accustomed to her astonishing us with her remembered and relearned abilities.

She became attached to her regular nurses and her therapists, and she was extremely comfortable with them, although, at times, she would still get confused remembering faces, mistaking one person for someone else on multiple occasions. It was like her brain would glitch on the details of facial recognition.

The staff on the eighth floor became fond of Sierra; they were amazed at her progress and often would stop by to say hello even when they were not scheduled with her that day. One nurse told us that whatever our family was doing spiritually, we keep going because it was working. She mentioned that it was almost like her healing was by God's hand. One doctor shared that he had never seen such a miraculous recovery in a TBI patient and that love was not a measurable treatment.

We played lots of games with her, which she loved. Her dogged determination to participate was a huge benefit. She wanted to be involved. There was a large sitting room at the end of the hall, where we would take Sierra to play games such as bean bag toss. Keeping her engaged in familiar activities and prayer was definitely working. We would pray with her every night and in the morning, too.

We shared all the gifts from her shrine with her, and she was fascinated that people sent her all these things. She would study each item as we told her who sent it and where it was from. The prayer cards were particularly interesting to her. There was one that really caught her attention; it was a photo of an older Saint Padre Pio. When I told her who it was, she shook her head. No.

I thought that was odd and light-heartedly argued that it was. She shook her head again. No. She said that it was not the Padre Pio who helped her come back. Come back? Dumbfounded, I Googled several pictures of Padre Pio when he was younger and found a picture of him when he was much younger, as a friar, in his mid-20s. I showed Sierra his picture.

"Is this who you met?" Sierra was absolute when she nodded yes.

I did not doubt her recollection and instantly thought of all the times I had prayed to him since I saw that video. All those times, I felt a warmth next to me. He had been there, interceding in Sierra's life. It made sense.

As the weeks progressed, so did her abilities. Her quiet warrior spirit was well and truly activated, and as we approached the end of September, Sierra was aware and alert and wanted to go home. She asked every day when she could leave. At that point, the earliest set date for her to come home was October 6, but she was still on a feeding tube, with a slow reintroduction of solids.

There was some talk of staying at Spaulding until she had the surgery to replace the piece of her skull, but we decided the best place for her to regain familiarity and remember her life was at home. The day before we left, they removed her feeding tube, and she was able to eat solids once again. We were elated for her.

Being able to chew and swallow food was another big step for Sierra's independence. We ordered the most delicious pizza from Regina's Pizzeria in the north end of Boston, and Sierra was delighted with the fact that she could indulge in tasting this masterpiece.

To be discharged from the hospital, Sierra had to go through an extensive exit evaluation. One of the doctors she met with was a psychotherapist we had not met before. When I first spoke with him, he had read Sierra's chart and asked me to prop up an iPad in front of her so he could conduct his exit interview.

I told him I would have to go get her as she was not immediately next to me. He didn't want me to put in too much effort stabilizing her, thinking she was in a wheelchair. I would have thought he had been expecting to meet someone who could barely speak or walk.

I chuckled to myself and told him it was no problem at all and he should see for himself how far Sierra had come in her recovery. He was amazed that she was walking and pronouncing words and sentences clearly and concisely. He was asking Sierra about current events and who was in the White House.

Without hesitation, she responded to President Trump. She even surprised us with the extent of her knowledge of current events, including COVID, which was only around a few months prior to her crash. After speaking with Sierra, he asked if she had a severe concussion. A concussion?

I had asked him if he reviewed her chart, but he had trouble reconciling the girl in front of him with her medical records from admission. He admittedly said he was going to "throw the books out on this one" as it made no sense to him the extent of her injuries and the girl he had just interviewed.

Her physical therapist noted she had more than exceeded the long-term goals set for her on that date. Sierra could now walk independently for six minutes at a speed of 2mph.

She could not maintain her balance while sitting yet due to her peripheral impairment from the severed left main facial nerve. There were also concerns about her lack of safety awareness and impulsivity. She would require supervision and ongoing PT to address her functional limitations and impairments, including balance, activity tolerance, gait mechanics, passive range of motion, posture, and coordination, as well as left-sided neglect, which was caused by the mid-brain stroke she had experienced.

She was still having difficulty controlling a writing instrument but was determined to regain that ability. Writing letters was a challenge, and she also had trouble with letter directionality. The language assessment noted that she was able to speak but had difficulty expressing her needs and understanding verbal information.

Sierra still had severe cognitive impairment disorientation, which meant she had an extremely tough time remembering things short-term, making decisions, concentrating, and retaining knowledge. She was still experiencing a post-traumatic confusion state. She was prescribed Ritalin, which was successful in helping her attention span.

Her test scores for the RBANS standard test (Repeatable Battery of the Assessment of Neuropsychological Status) yielded extremely low scores all around. She had little verbal or visual memory and low scores on expressive vocabulary and verbal fluency. The medical exit report was harsh, but we knew her journey was not over. She had come a long way, and her journey had only just begun.

Her recovery over the previous eight weeks had been nothing short of miraculous and more than any of the trained medical professionals had expected, but she would still need months of ongoing physical, mental, and speech therapy. She was no longer in a vegetative state, but she still had so far to go. We were up for the task; I knew if God had brought her this far, he would not be deserting us now.

We envisioned and prayed for a complete recovery for Sierra. There was no doubt in our minds. It was just a matter of doing the work, completing the therapies, and keeping the faith.

When she would get frustrated, I would remind her, "It won't always be like this," because I knew it wouldn't.

On Tuesday, October 6th, Sierra was discharged from Spaulding Rehabilitation Hospital. It was a beautiful day, and most of our family was there in our #SierraStrong shirts to bring her home. The staff had gathered to congratulate Sierra with a song and send-off.

A wheelchair had been ordered by her doctors, but it was not necessary; Sierra did not need it. This moment was so miraculous. I reflected on the memory of when Steven heard Sierra say, "I love you." Steven was convinced Sierra would not only recover but would walk out of Spaulding on her own with no assistance, feeding tubes, or trach. And she did. We filmed her walking out of Spaulding when, only two months earlier, she had arrived in a vegetative state, not even able to hold up her head.

I posted the event on the Miracle for Sierra Facebook page for that day's update, and she received so much love and many promises of continued prayer support. People were inspired by her progress, calling it a miracle. We agreed, and I was touched; so many people were still so invested in Sierra's progress. The group was incredibly supportive of us and each other, and we still received messages from all over the United States and the world.

Amy Jones Longmoore

October 6, 2020.

Day 91: "I believe in miracles because I am one because there is no doubt in my mind that I am only here today because of God's grace and mercy. I am not ashamed of the one who saved my soul."

On the way home, we stopped at McDonald's for a chocolate shake. Sierra had been excited to get one, and we were happy to indulge her request. As we drove through town and got closer to home, we pointed out all the #SierraStrong signs that were still in people's yards. She thought it was great but did not fully comprehend it was all for her.

When she got home, she was so happy to be back with the family and in familiar surroundings that she visibly relaxed. Sierra was also delighted to see her favorite cat, Milo, who had remained on her bed for months, faithfully waiting for her to return. Seeing the change in Sierra almost immediately, we knew we had made the right decision to bring her home.

The very next day, there was a double rainbow right over our home, which we took as a positive sign from above that we were on the right path.

Even though it was a relief for her and our family to have her at home, it was incredibly challenging. Sierra was still wearing her helmet to protect her brain, which still was missing a portion of her skull, and one of us had to be with her all the time. She was still having trouble controlling her body. She was also still incontinent and required bathroom and other personal care assistance. We installed grab bars in the shower and had a shower chair for her.

I had to develop step-by-step processes for her to relearn regular routines. I printed checklists of her morning and evening routines, and I would mark them off with dry-erase markers. It was not just that she had to be supervised; someone had to be with her 24/7 to ensure she was safe and to show her and teach her how to live and take care of herself.

Sierra could speak, but she still had difficulty expressing her needs and understanding verbal information. She could answer yes and no, but often it was impulsive. She could understand and follow one-step commands, but she was very easily distracted. Her attention span was increasing, just a few seconds more every day. Sometimes, she could remain focused for almost four minutes, and this was becoming noticeably longer week over week.

In having to revisit every stage in her life again, Sierra had to relearn every little thing. From remembering how to use a fork to how to open the door, pulling up her own covers, and washing her face, there were moments of frustration and tears, but she was determined to master all the skills she knew before.

Her memories returned in waves, which would reinvigorate her, and she was never down for long. We all found her focus and motivation inspiring, and as a family, we backed her and wanted her to succeed.

The school had gone back a month before, and it was the girls' senior year. Aspen and Sierra had spoken of and planned this year since middle school together. They would talk about the classes they would take and sports they would play, dances they would go to, and, of course, prom and graduation. What should have been the beginning of an exciting new phase for them was not even close to what either of them had imagined.

Aspen was devastated that her twin was not able to join her at school as a senior. It was important for her to keep Sierra included in all the activities and fun of the senior year that they had talked about. The first one was painting her parking spot. Aspen and her Uncle Joe spent a day painting Sierra's parking spot, which was a privilege for all seniors.

The words "Family Forever" became our mantra and were painted underneath the mighty tree that sprawled branches of strength and encouragement. Aspen would also tell Sierra everything that happened at school and in class every single day when she came home. She did not want Sierra to miss a thing.

A local business, The Newbury Village Store, made a "Welcome Home" cake for her, which was a celebratory surprise. The first Sunday she was home, we all went to church together. We had been part of the parish for years, with each child being baptized and making the sacraments of communion and confirmation there. They had lifted us up in prayer continuously since the day of the crash in July. Going to church that day felt like a homecoming for us; it was a joyous occasion.

With all the excitement in the community, it took no time at all for Sierra's ex to discover she was back at home. This fueled his desire for contact with her. He would often park on our street or drive slowly past our house, loudly revving his car's engine. If he did not have such a menacing presence, it would have been laughable. But it was just a nuisance and often felt like we were stuck in some weird stalker movie.

All these things combined had the desired effect on Sierra's memories. Even if she did not have complete recall yet, the familiarity was comforting, and little by little, she was becoming surer of herself. She did, however, have a very clear recall of the abuse she had experienced from her ex. Having never experienced anything like that before, and of the crash. It was like the memory of the thoughts and anxiety she was feeling at the time she left the road had solidified in her mind. These memories would haunt her; she was terrified he would try to hurt her family, too.

Chapter Six – One Day at a Time

[4] Love suffers long *and* is kind; love does not envy; love does not parade itself, is not puffed up; [5] does not behave rudely, does not seek its own, is not provoked, thinks no evil; [6] does not rejoice in iniquity, but rejoices in the truth; [7] bears all things, believes all things, hopes all things, endures all things. 1 Corinthians 13:4-7

Wanting to continue the momentum she had built at Spaulding, we had scheduled Sierra's therapies to begin the day after she returned home. Her first night back in her own bed, with her cat Milo back on her bed purring all night, was peaceful. It felt good to have her home. The next day, Steven, Sierra, and I headed to Dartmouth to meet with her new therapists.

While we were in the waiting room, we were joined by a mother and son. I thought she seemed familiar, but I could not place her. I did not give it too much thought as we were called into the appointment to meet the new team of therapists.

During our journey until that point with Sierra, I had met dozens of people online and over the phone and spoken to so many incredibly selfless women who had reached out to share their own stories of the traumatic brain injuries their children had experienced. I was touched by the support from strangers and humbled at how generous of spirit they were.

One area mother, in particular, named Maria, had taken a lot of time to talk me through the many scary and doubt-ridden moments we had experienced with Sierra. Her son, Peter, had sustained a severe TBI during his freshman year of college. Even though I had spoken to her often and at length on the phone and through social media since mid-July, we had never met in person.

Sierra's new therapists were very friendly and upbeat. We were introduced to Danielle, her speech therapist; Maxwell, her physical therapist; and Jen, her occupational therapist. All three of them were astounded at how much she had progressed in such a short amount of time.

After meeting her new therapists and discussing each therapy and treatment goal, they gave us a short tour of the rooms and showed us the tools they would be using while working with Sierra.

Then they started, preferring to get straight into it. Sierra's first therapy was with Danielle, and we headed to her office where she did speech therapy, followed by the gym that was filled with all sorts of equipment with Maxwell for physical therapy, then finished this shorter session with Jen in the occupational therapy room that even included a kitchen to help with everyday tasks. They were all very encouraging and set big goals with Sierra. This was very inspiring for her, and she was excited to get started. It was an incredibly positive start to Sierra's next phase of treatment; all three of her therapists were confident and had very high energy. We felt good about the work she had ahead of her.

When the therapy session with Sierra ended, the lady in the waiting room introduced herself to us as we were walking out, asking if it was us and explaining how she knew us. Her name and her son's name were familiar to Steven and us, as I always shared with him the names and details of conversations I had with different people and the advice they offered. When we finished the session, Maria came over and officially introduced herself and her son Peter to Sierra and me.

It was wonderful to meet face to face. I could finally say thank you. Sierra and Peter finally had a chance to connect. We hugged and agreed to stay in touch in person, comforted that we had made new friends who knew exactly what we were each going through. Maria told me later that after meeting Sierra, Peter had taken more steps than he had before, inspired by meeting a new friend who had experienced a similar injury.

It was genuine connections like this that highlighted our days and gave me insight into the way God uses other people's words and actions to provide the support needed for the people who need it. Often, people would send me messages on social media that began along the lines of, 'I don't usually reach out to people this way, but something compelled me to share....' I know this is God's way of assisting us.

Almost as soon as she got home from Spaulding, Sierra started talking about graduating with Aspen and her class. There were mixed opinions from the medical professionals working with

Sierra concerning this idea. Most of her therapists advised against it because they thought it would affect her physical progress and medical benefits.

She was gaining, but she still struggled with word-finding and tended to get stuck on certain words or phrases. Speech comprehension was also still an issue, but Steven and I decided not to shut the door on that option and leave that decision up to Sierra. We knew she would let us know what she was ready for and when she wanted to do it.

The day after that, we took Sierra to see Father Sam at Dartmouth Hitchcock Medical Center, who had also been instrumental in leading a huge local prayer movement for Sierra and our family. We knew he had to see her.

He was so overcome with joy at seeing her walking and talking that he insisted we immediately go with him to the PICU to show the staff what a miracle we had been blessed with. COVID restrictions were still enforced, but Fr. Sam knew what he had to do. We followed him to the PICU.

As we walked into the PICU ward at Dartmouth, it was a strange feeling, considering where we had left there just two months ago. The situation was vastly different. Sierra had been in a vegetative state, and we did not know what was going to happen. We were told we would be lucky if one day she could brush her teeth on her own when we left, never mind walk or talk. As we walked with Fr. Sam, after the initial ripple of realization, you could hear a pin drop. The ward activity ground to a halt as the staff stared at her like she was a ghost.

The reality that this was Sierra Longmoore, the girl who had been in the terrible crash and suffered massive brain trauma just a few short months ago, made multiple nurses clap and cheer. A couple even ran over to hug her, so amazed to see her walking and talking. One of them cried as she watched Sierra walk unassisted with us. The rest of them stood frozen to the spot, amazed to see her. There was barely a dry eye as we walked through the hall. It was an emotional moment for all of us.

The doctor who had advised us to have Sierra's last rites given on July 14th was completely dumbstruck, and she teared up with the realization that Sierra was blessed with a miracle. She and her team did not think Sierra would live through the night just a short time ago. At that moment, seeing their tears of relief and joy, I realized how hard it must be for the medical staff of a pediatric intensive care department to see so many injured children who are not as lucky as Sierra. It must be heartwarming for them to witness this kind of miracle.

It was an emotional yet uplifting visit, and it gave Sierra a deeper insight into the community of medical professionals who had been around her constantly, taking care of her while she was in a coma. She was amazed and touched that so many people she didn't know were so happy to see her.

Sierra continued to attend multiple outpatient therapies five days a week.

Just two days before major surgery, we attended Aspen's senior soccer game at the high school. Our family and extended family all proudly wore our #Sierrastrong t-shirts and made signs in support of Aspen's big game. This was the first appearance Sierra had made at a community event since coming home from Spaulding. The team had graced her with a bouquet of flowers and invited her to the field for team pictures. But the highlight of the game was when Aspen looked at Sierra as she ran down the field and said, "This goal is for you." Then she forcefully kicked the soccer ball past the goalie into the net!

We headed back to Dartmouth Hitchcock Medical Center again on October 16th. The operation to put the missing piece of her entire front skull back in that had been rain-checked at the beginning of September was rescheduled for Lindsay's birthday. I could not help but feel these recurring big moments of action for Sierra's treatments coinciding with family members' birthdays were more divine intervention. However, the fact that Steven and I had been stretched psychologically since the day of her crash in July unexpectedly revisited us with a vengeance as we met with Dr. Ball to discover if the section of Sierra's skull that had been defrosted for the first scheduled operation was viable.

This had weighed heavily in the back of my mind since that day weeks ago when the procedure was canceled. What would happen if the large piece of skull that had been defrosted was unable to be used? What would happen to the open area in her head? Would she ever not have to wear the bulky helmet that protected her brain? My thoughts were like a runaway train. I knew that words are powerful; however, I did not dare express any of them. As Steven and I gripped each other's hands in the surgeon's office, I knew he had the same fears.

When Dr. Ball told us her bone looked good and was able to be used in her operation, the relief washed over us like a wave. I felt all that tension drain out of us. That was short-lived, however, as we signed the appropriate waivers, releasing them from any liability in case one of a multitude of things that could go wrong during the operation happened, including her death.

By then, Steven and I were extremely exhausted and emotionally fatigued. We realized that the months of extreme stress, worry, and doubt had taken a toll on us. We went to the chapel and prayed together, as we had so often when she was in a coma. Being able to pull together in prayer as a couple had given us so much strength and resilience. We knew God was watching, and we trusted in His plan, even if we did not understand it at times.

We did not know yet, but since the craniotomy had been performed three months beforehand, Sierra's body had developed a calcified bone layer under the skin to protect her brain. This could pose a problem in her healing, but her skull was successfully reattached. Again, it was a textbook operation, and once again, we were grateful to have such a highly skilled and experienced surgeon and his team working on Sierra.

When the operation had been completed, she was taken to the same room that she had spent almost five weeks in after the crash for recovery. This was surreal and unsettling for us, although we knew she would only be in here for a few days; it was still the room.

As we sat in that room, I remembered the thirty-four days Steven and I had lived there, keeping vigil at her bedside. We remembered in vivid detail the posters and pictures, the flowers and cards, the makeshift shrine on the windowsill, the angel light that had turned on by itself, and, of course, vigilantly keeping watch over the machines that were keeping her alive, monitoring every beep and tone unconsciously, taking turns to nap. One of us was continually on alert, watching over our daughter. It seemed like a lifetime ago, yet it was only months.

And now, the room was empty. It was just a regular hospital room. We could turn on the television and watch Sierra's favorite shows with her. We could order meals with her and for her, and we knew she would be walking out with us. This feeling alone was very gratifying and renewed our faith that God was watching over her. I started to have more insight into the possibility that he had a bigger purpose for our girl.

We consciously chose to view it positively as a revisiting of the place where her life had been saved, and she came back to us. It was a blessing. My mind often returned to what I had said to Sierra since the beginning of her healing journey, 'it won't always be like this.' I reminded myself of how far Sierra had come to even get to this point, and we knew she would continue to progress.

Sierra had no memory of being in that room in Dartmouth, so it was bittersweet only for us. While she was in recovery, she had a few visitors: three of her nurses who had been her main nursing staff while in a coma – Leah, Charlie, and Sean all came to see her over those few days. They were so overjoyed to see her and hear of her progress thus far.

She was happy that people were visiting her and was very sweet to them, but she did not know who they were. To us, they were angels in disguise. The care, love, and attention they gave to Sierra was unwavering. Steven and I came to know them very well, and likewise us to them. Their respect and dignity for what we were going through echoed in their graceful care for Sierra.

After the operation, her face was swollen because of the extra fluid from her body's response to reabsorbing the calcified layer that had grown to protect her brain. She had to have ice packs on her eyes, which were also swollen shut. Because she could not see, she could not return to therapy until she was reevaluated.

After three days, she was cleared, and we checked her out of Dartmouth PICU for the last time and headed home. The day after we returned home, Sierra received another beautiful gift in the mail from The Home Depot associate in New Mexico who had been following Sierra's journey since the week of the crash.

It was the symbol of 'God is Greater than our Highs and Lows' hand-painted on a t-shirt. It was colorful and vibrant, and Sierra was touched that someone had sent her something so beautiful. She was always so grateful and excited to receive gifts in the mail and would insist on sending a thank-you letter, card, or painting back.

After the operation, we noticed that her awareness of things she had already learned had slipped, and there were many things she had to get reacquainted with again. This was a little disheartening, as we had originally been told that once the bone was replaced (while still at Spaulding), she would progress much quicker.

However, that was weeks ago, and her body did not wait to start the healing process. The calcified layer, which was a natural part of healing, was also the main hindrance in her progress now, but we held on to the hope that if she had already relearned these skills so recently, she would be able to do it again. Her brain and body would continue to heal.

We returned to Dartmouth for a checkup a few days later, and it was the first time I got to see the staples and the incision. Sierra was half bald. They had shaved her head from ear to ear across the crown of her head to reattach her skull, and there were sixty-four staples in her head, which was graphic and harrowing for a mother to see on her own child. I knew what they had done, but up until that point, I had not seen what they had done.

The reports were incredibly positive; however, Sierra did not suffer from any tissue rejection, and her skull had started healing the way it should. With the antibiotics she was taking, her recovery was going very well. She also did not suffer from migraines or even headaches, which we were told could be expected as they were a normal side effect of a healing brain, especially one that had been as injured as hers.

Sierra was given the all-clear to get back to therapy a week after the operation. The left side of her face still had minimal movement due to the severed facial nerve from the crash. But she was excited for the swelling to reduce enough for her to get back to therapy to continue her healing journey.

As the days went by, Sierra worked hard learning her lower-level Activities of Daily Living Skills (ADLS) like bathing, dressing, getting out of bed, using the toilet, eating using different utensils, etc. All day-to-day activities take multiple steps to complete. She was given an initial estimated period of twelve weeks to master those skills before moving on to higher-level ADLS like folding laundry, grocery shopping, personal finances, etc.

Much to her therapists' surprise and Sierra's satisfaction, she mastered the lower-level skills in four weeks. We were all still praying. The support on the Facebook page was still growing. Sierra was determined to get back to the self she remembered. She was unstoppable.

One weekend at the beginning of Fall, we took her up to her grandparents' land to show her the healing garden that had been planted in her honor. She spent a long time walking around it, taking it all in. Watching her so innocently realizing that it was all done for her was touching. Again, this reminds us of her experiencing big emotions and learning the various skills to navigate them for the first time. Like she had done only a decade or so before, it was interesting that now she was relearning things from closer to her age. She was catching up quickly. It was still remarkable to witness.

Steven and I were so thankful to be together as a family and to have Sierra on the path of recovery. The dynamic of our family was irrevocably altered, and so was the trajectory of our twins' lives. But we knew it was all part of God's plan for our family. We held no anger or grief towards God. But witnessing the compulsive behavior of Sierra's exes, we started to question his role in this whole thing.

The texts and Sierra's phone records had revealed some very disturbing information, and Steven and I were unsure of how to rid our daughter of this unwanted attention. Our family had blocked him on our social media accounts early on, but he created fake accounts and sent us disconcerting private messages as well as letters in the mail. We had filed a No Trespass Order with the county courthouse, hoping to put a stop to his obsessive behavior.

Steven recounted Sierra's first words to him when she spoke for the first time. Struggling to pronounce the words, "I love you," then, "He hit me." At the time, it did not make sense.

It was beginning to look increasingly like it was not a single-car crash. A witness had come forward, reporting seeing a car matching his friend's following her white SUV remarkably close on Snake Rd the morning of her crash. It stood out in their mind because they were driving too fast for the twists and turns of the road.

Her phone records indicated he had sent her multiple threatening texts before the crash, as well as that twenty-six-minute phone call. What we had initially assumed to be an ex-boyfriend in shock in those first few days was him just trying to find out what she was saying about the crash.

Despite the No Trespass order, he would park at the end of our driveway, wanting "to talk." It was never clear exactly who he wanted to talk to; there was nothing anyone had to say to him, and the police were called every time. He was fixated. We continued to pray, not wanting to waste any energy on someone else's issues, knowing that God keeps score and that it was not up to us to seek revenge.

We had done what we could with the authorities, and our daughter needed our strength and positivity, not our thoughts of vengeance on some lost soul. We also know that once a person's thoughts turn toward revenge and retribution, the enemy has won. We kept our eyes firmly on the Lord Almighty.

Continuing to focus on Sierra and her recovery took all our energy; she was working extremely hard in her therapies, and with each new milestone, we could start her on something else. It was important for her to regain control of her facial muscles and gross motor skills, which included kicking, climbing, bending, throwing, pushing, bouncing, dancing, and scooting (yes, scooting is a valuable locomotive activity to master).

Her speech therapy was also progressing well. She met with her therapist twice a week, once in person and once remotely. Her biggest challenges are still related to her memory and executive functioning. She struggled with organizing her thoughts, which affected her clarity of expression; giving descriptions was difficult, and she also struggled with word-finding.

Although she benefited from phonemic clues, such as having the first letter of a word to trigger her memory, this increased her ability to pull information from her memory. We realized that she is a visual learner and started to find ways to color-code notes to help her organize her schedule.

As Sierra had been shy and introverted her whole life, she was always reserved around people she did not know. However, since her injury, she had to meet an enormous number of new people, which increased her social apprehension. Although that aspect of her personality remained relatively unchanged, her sweet and caring side seemed to have been intensified by the crash.

In fact, we noticed that all her emotions and behaviors had intensified, including her sensory experiences, such as tolerance of hot and cold or annoying and repetitive sounds. She was fearful for her safety and always wanted a family member with her outside of the home.

Previously an emotionally strong and resilient young lady, since the crash and along her recovery, Sierra had started showing signs of PTSD, which is completely normal for TBI patients. We started her in counseling at the Center for Integrative Health to be able to address some of this.

Because her left facial nerve had been severed, her left eye looked quite different from her right, and the left side of her face was hard to control because of the trauma. She also began vision rehab appointments with specialists in Boston, along with her normal therapies, and she started facial therapy at a Massachusetts eye and ear clinic.

The neuro-ophthalmologist we were working with was convinced she could help Sierra neurologically retrain her eyes to correct her peripheral vision, convergence of her eyes (where the eyes do not move together as they look at objects closely), and double vision.

We were grateful that, despite the apparently irreparable damage to her left-side optic nerve and multiple predictions of blindness in her left eye, her vision had been spared. She had regular visits with a neuro-ophthalmologist, an optometrist, and a vision specialist. She was prescribed prism glasses, which corrected double vision, making it easier for her to focus on objects with both eyes.

Sierra had also lost numerous teeth in the crash due to the impact of her face onto the steering wheel. So, in November, Sierra also started dental treatment with root canals and caps to replace her missing teeth.

Every day was hard work for Sierra, but she was full of determination to retain the information and access her previous memories and skills. At times, she was exhausted and impatient with herself, but she never gave up. She would doggedly keep going, and her warrior spirit was an inspiration to us all.

Chapter Seven – Love Is Action

[11] For by me your days will be multiplied,
And years of life will be added to you. Proverbs 9:11

Within a few days of Sierra's crash, the #SierraStrong movement was gaining momentum in our local area, with yard signs and t-shirts appearing all around our home county of Orange, Vermont. This was on our periphery at first. Lindsay had partnered with a few other locals, and they were busy printing and selling signs, t-shirts, and bracelets by the boxful to area businesses and sports teams.

Due to the ongoing COVID restrictions, they would meet at rest stops or outside diners to distribute them far and wide. This garnered the interest of local news outlets interested in the story behind the #SierraStrong hashtag and Sierra's journey.

Jim Kenyon, the columnist from Valley News, first wrote a feature story about Sierra and the Sierra Strong movement a mere week after the crash. This helped raise awareness for Sierra's fight, the fundraising that had already begun to help our family and the community support that was assisting us on our toughest days. As she was still in a coma at the time, we appreciated the positivity this generated.

Jim Kenyon also wrote a follow-up opinion piece for the Valley News in September 2020, detailing her miraculous journey up to that point. Although he was never a Facebook person, he personally had been following Sierra's journey via the "Miracle for Sierra - God's Heroes Unite" Facebook page that I had started the week after the crash to keep people updated with her journey. By September, the page had almost 3,500 followers and continued to grow.

We had interest from other area publications and media as well. The Caledonian Record interviewed Sierra, Aspen, and me in February 2021. There were follow-up articles where she was featured in Dartmouth Hospital's regular "Our Patients. Their Stories" section as well.

The "Miracle for Sierra - God's Heroes Unite" Facebook page was an important tool for so many reasons: personally, it was important for me to keep an accurate record of Sierra's progress. Keeping track of the small daily wins was cathartic and inspiring for us.

Often, in the middle of something overwhelming, it is difficult to retain perspective of how far you have come. We were blessed to have a few trusted people work as our liaisons within the Home Depot and school communities. It was still so easy for stories to be made up and spread around, and I did my best to keep that to a minimum.

There was also outstanding support from teachers and staff at her high school. The Oxbow High School counseling coordinator, Lomond Richardson, stepped up and was instrumental in the role of liaison between us and the school community, which was greatly appreciated. The high school started using its electronic message board to post the Sierra Strong message and updates about her progress for the entire community.

There were many unexpected and touching gestures from local businesses, too. Youngs Photography, a local Newbury photography business, rallied dozens of people who posed in their Sierra Strong t-shirts, making a human chain with blue ribbons that read "Sierra Strong," and took a photo by drone, which they sent to us while she was still at Dartmouth, which we added to her wall of love and inspiration. When she was well enough to understand that all these people had done that for her, it became one of Sierra's favorite photos.

A local youth baseball team printed #SierraStrong on their jerseys and hats in support of our daughter. It was encouraging to know that so many people were invested in Sierra's recovery. There was not a moment of doubt that she would not make it, and the miracles we witnessed on her journey only confirmed our faith that we serve a powerful God.

Newbury Village Store collected donations for Sierra, too, wanting to do their part to help lift our family's increasing financial burden. Melissa, one of the store owners, followed Sierra's progress on Facebook and, wanting to help, thought it seemed like the best thing to do. She was familiar with our family from our time in the area and knew we must be facing ongoing travel expenses. Her practical nature wanted to help provide gas money for family members to get to and from the hospital daily.

It felt like we were blessed by our community every day. In the weeks after we arrived home with Sierra and our immediate family returned to their regular pre-crash routines, I had assumed the support for Sierra would dissipate once she was out of the hospital, but it did not.

I was filled with awe that it kept flowing. From further afield, the gifts and messages of love and support were still pouring in. This often motivated both Sierra and me as we became even closer. Our previously strong bond reached new levels.

Although the reality was it was still a lot of hard work. I was Sierra's main caregiver and with her 24/7. I was her driver and her nurse, her assistant, her cheer squad, and her coach, keeping her on track and motivated every morning, noon, and night. Sierra was also working hard; she had a very full and robust schedule, busy every day from morning until night.

My sole purpose at that time was her. Getting her to her appointments, along with helping her relearn the daily essentials, became my entire life. It was also imperative she had quality rest and sleep every night to help heal her brain.

She was such a trooper, but there were some days she didn't want to leave the house, go to therapy, or workout, and I would have to remind her of how far she had come and how inspiring she was to others. It wouldn't always be like this, and we would not give up. So, she couldn't either.

We did everything we could think of to reinforce what she was learning. We printed her morning and evening routines, along with her daily therapy schedules, and had them in sheet protectors so we could mark off her tasks as we went along with her schedule. This helped offer her a visual for each part of each day, and as her short-term memory was getting stronger, cues like this solidified routines and habits for her.

Some days were good, and some days were not so good, but there was no question she was gaining strength, confidence, and skills each week. Sierra was not the only one experiencing such life changes; personally, my own faith deepened, and I became more reliant on our Heavenly Father than I had ever been before, taking time in the mornings to wake earlier than everyone else and pray. Steven also practiced this routine.

Even though there were times when Steven and I were aware of how drained we were, we were both more aware of our other children's need for their mother and father, too, not just Sierra. We were very conscious that at thirteen, our youngest son Tanner had experienced such growth and development during the summer when we were absent so much of the time.

Aspen was a senior in high school and had all sorts of activities and events going on, and while we were grateful that our two eldest were independent and easily took on the responsibility of the house and their little brother, it bothered us that we were not as accessible for them as we once had been. The dynamic of our family had evolved and changed, with Lindsay and Tristan and our extended family stepping in to support and take responsibility for so many things, which we were thankful for.

We were still overcome with moments of incredible mom guilt and dad guilt that things were not the way we had envisioned for any of us. And we could not be everything to everyone as we had previously been able to.

As Sierra's mom, I was one of her role models, and being strong was my only option. It took a long time until I acknowledged my own mental health. Almost two and a half years passed until I sought therapy for the PTSD I experienced from the day of the crash and the months afterward.

At the time, I reminded myself often that God saves his biggest battles for his strongest warriors, and I gained a lot of strength from my daily devotions. Holding it together became second nature for me, a mixture of survivor's guilt and exhaustion. I was grateful for all that I had but occasionally would wonder how I could keep going or if I even had the right to feel the way I did. But I was also proud of the changes I saw in my immediate family; we were different but more cohesive as a supportive unit, and the lines and roles had blurred.

As she healed, we became acquainted with the new Sierra. Her personality was altered, and although she was still essentially the same Sierra, she was also irrevocably changed in so many ways. The mannerisms and quirks that made her our Sierra were somewhat gone, and at times, it was challenging for all concerned.

We have been told by numerous doctors and therapists that when someone has experienced TBI, depending on the location of the damage, their personality can be permanently altered. We had initially been concerned as she had experienced so much damage to the area of the brain believed to control personality. But Sierra became the complete opposite. God chose her for a different purpose.

She was very loving, concerned, and compassionate, wanting to reach out and love everybody going through difficulty, even if it was just an inconvenience like dropping a pen. This bonded her to many of her therapists and the professionals who worked with her. We often heard how she was such a breeze to work with, as she was motivated and sweet to everyone.

As Sierra regained her memory and became cognizant of all the prayers and support that had been and were continually directed towards her, she wanted to personally acknowledge the attention. So, near the end of October, Steven, his dad, and Sierra drove around town and took photos of her in front of all the businesses that had supported her and still had signs that read "Sierra Strong."

We posted all of these on the Miracle for Sierra Facebook page, thanking everyone who remembered our family during such a difficult time. She posed proudly in a strong man bicep curl, which became the symbol of the strength of her spirit.

Right from the beginning of the page, I vowed to share her story every step of the way – good and bad – no matter the outcome. Social media was our connection to the world, and the world connected back. People from across the U.S. and the globe joined the prayer group to pray for her recovery journey. Her story was shared on Twitter, Instagram, Snapchat, and YouTube. I continued to share the daily updates, which had become as much of a lifeline to me as to some of the people who had connected to her journey.

We started to hear the most wonderful stories of people who had lost hope during COVID but who were now invested in Sierra's recovery and became solid prayer warriors, giving themselves a higher purpose and establishing (or re-establishing) a meaningful connection with God. This was an unintended result but, again, made perfect sense when seeing God's bigger plan, and I was happy to be able to provide the catalyst by way of daily updates for people to rediscover their faith. It was gratifying to see how these people connected with each other in shows of genuine support, too.

I was continually inspired by the people we met online who selflessly offered their heartfelt ideas, thoughts, and prayers. I became aware of Sierra's story, bringing people together and bonding us with new local people as well. I often received messages of hope and inspiration on Facebook and other social media channels, with people sharing their own recovery stories and journeys.

We even made some new local friends: Walter Way, an elderly local gentleman who, at 85 years old, had been widowed a couple of years beforehand and was told about Sierra a few days after the crash. He became interested in her story, as it seemed so tragic at the outset. Walt was not a devout Catholic as his wife had been, but he did believe, and he started to pray for Sierra and her recovery.

He quickly became dedicated to following her journey and celebrating each of her milestones along with us. He regularly messaged me with words of support and kindness, which were truly appreciated. There was no hidden agenda, just a genuine intention for Sierra's recovery. His kind words bonded him to our family, and he became a regular supporter of Sierra on social media as well as in real life. Walt knew my in-laws from being local for a long time, but he became close to our family and has remained a family friend.

Amongst our messages of support, Steven and I would often receive recommendations from friends and acquaintances of movies and documentaries we should watch or podcasts we should listen to. One movie that kept being suggested was "Fatima," the story of the three shepherd children who saw apparitions of the Blessed Mother Mary in Marian, Portugal, in 1917. Besides the fact that Mary had always been significant in our lives, we felt compelled to view it with Sierra sometime soon. However, with the busyness of life, we took a while to get to it.

On February 13, 2021, as we were driving through Newbury, we were captivated by a full 360-degree sunbow around the sun. None of us had ever seen one before, and it was so out of the ordinary that we pulled the car off the road to observe it and take pictures.

We were spellbound, and it was visible for the rest of the drive home. To us, it was another miraculous sign that God was with us and Sierra was being watched over in her healing journey. That night, we finally got to sit down as a family and watch the movie "Fatima," and you can imagine our delight and surprise when the three children of Fatima asked Mary for a sign to prove to the townspeople that she had really appeared to them.

The sign was a beautiful, brilliant sunbow. Our Lady appeared and spoke to the children on the 13th day of each month. I had initially been impressed that we got to witness yet another incredible rainbow, but seeing the tie into the movie and Mother Mary filled me with renewed faith that Sierra's healing journey was not complete.

After we watched the movie, I went back to the photos we took that afternoon on our way home and was interested in seeing what our local community made of it. I checked our local Facebook pages. Our community is very weather-aware, and anytime there were spectacular clouds or beautiful atmospheric events, there would always be many photos and posts about them, often within minutes.

To my surprise, there was not one single photo, post, or mention of the glorious sunbow we had witnessed on the way home that afternoon. I even called my mother-in-law and daughter Lindsay to see if they had noticed it. Nobody had. It appeared we were the only ones who had seen it.

Sierra started to think even more about the people who had helped her since the crash. She was curious about all the people who had helped her, and it became important to her to thank the first responders who had been first on the scene on the day. She knew there were twenty-three first responders who had been there, most of them volunteers, and she started thinking of the best way to say thank you to that community. She wanted them to know how grateful she was because, without them, she would not have survived. She owed them her life. The idea of a party for all of them during EMS Week was born.

Chapter Eight – Warrior Spirit

> 27 The LORD *is* my light and my salvation;
> Whom shall I fear?
> The LORD *is* the strength of my life;
> Of whom shall I be afraid? Psalms 27:1

Right from the beginning, Sierra was a miracle child; she and her twin sister, Aspen, were born at 26 weeks (about 6 months) gestation, making an emergency entrance into the world on December 17th, 2002, weighing barely over three pounds each at birth.

My water broke on December 8th (my dad's birthday). We quickly learned that Sierra's sac was the one leaking amniotic fluid, and as a result, I was put on bed rest for two weeks, waiting for my white blood cell count to increase so they could be delivered via C-section. This gave us early insight into the fighting spirit and the force to reckon with that Sierra was going to be. She was shaking up our world before she physically came into it.

When the girls were born a few weeks later, they spent five weeks together in the NICU. And even though we were able to bring Sierra home first, after about a week, one morning, I noticed her little body was blue. She was rushed to a nearby hospital, and from there, she was taken by helicopter to Dartmouth Hitchcock Medical Center. I will never forget that morning when the doctors told me she only had about an hour to live.

They said the swift actions of getting her to the hospital saved her life. Sierra was found to have sepsis and spent a week in the pediatric ICU. She was so small that her whole body fit on the width of the pillow. Thankfully, she recovered with no lasting health problems.

As they grew, Sierra was a reserved and quiet child. She was extremely introverted but had a poised, fierce energy about her. She would always take a stand for what she believed in. No matter how small she was in size, her personality was larger than any room she was in. Sierra was a leader. She was not one to follow a crowd or pretend to be somebody she wasn't to fit in. She had her own style and marched to the beat of her drum from a young age. I am proud of various characteristics that inspire me in all my children, and it is Sierra's fierce independence that I admire most about her.

Throughout their childhood, the girls were inseparable. Sharing the special connection that twins experience, their bond is often unexplainable. In elementary school, they were placed in different classes, which allowed them to form different friend groups and grow as individuals. But outside of school, they remained the best of friends. Every birthday was a marvelous event, as both girls had a lot of friends, and there were always two different cakes! One year, we invited their entire first and second-grade combined classes for a pizza party. Sierra insisted on having a pirate cake, while Aspen had a princess cake. Their choices summed them up perfectly.

Sierra was a responsible child and took charge of different chores around the house from an early age. Her work ethic was admirable, whether at home, at school, or in sports. Her commitment to her activities ensured Sierra played varsity-level sports as a freshman in high school. Her commitment was part of her very fiber, and it carried her well as she grew. She believed she could make a difference and showed up with 100% conviction and purpose in everything she did.

Sierra was also very creative and would paint and draw incredible artwork to give away as gifts. A particularly notable painting she did had been inspired by Thomas Kincade. After connecting with his story, we had it framed, and it still hangs in our home today. Sierra always had a love for animals, too, especially cats. We had many family pets in our home: three dogs and three cats in total.

She loved them all, but two of the cats were Sierra's. She fed them and changed their litter boxes religiously, taking her responsibility for them very seriously. They would follow her around the house, and while she was away from home for the weeks after the crash, as previously mentioned, one of them spent the whole time on her bed, only leaving to eat and use the litter box.

Like most parents, my husband and I always want our children to be safe and happy, and when someone or something hurts them, it hurts us deeply, too.

It is best summed up in Elizabeth Stone's quote: "The decision to have a child – it is momentous. It is to decide forever to have your heart go walking around outside your body."

This is perhaps the most accurate summary of the depth of parenthood. I am sure almost every parent can attest to the heartbreak of watching their children grow and learn life's harsh lessons.

I remember when Sierra was in Fourth Grade, she wanted to cut her long hair off and try a pixie cut, which was very short around the ears and wispy at the back. It was a bold change, and we all adored it; she looked amazing. But it did not take long for the meaner kids at school to make fun of her super shortcut, so different from all the other girls' hair, and they started bullying her by calling her a boy and other derogatory names. I remember how demoralized this made Sierra, and it broke my heart.

We talked about bullying with Sierra and our other children, and she came to understand that the problem was theirs, not hers. Her strong spirit prevailed, and she would never let anyone at school see they got the best of her. Her real feelings were saved for the safety of her home.

But she was usually very upbeat and bounced back quickly from any setbacks. Sierra was the most introverted twin, but as the eldest twin in a family of five children, she always considered herself "the middle child."

The middle children are the ones who are ignored or neglected because of birth order; they are not able to have the rights of the eldest or get away with as much as the youngest. Although being the middle child has its own perks, often being included in the activities and conversations with the elder siblings and looked up to by the younger siblings. The middle child ends up with the best of both worlds.

Sierra loved the great outdoors, and being with her immediate and extended family, she would gladly seize the opportunity to spend time with loved ones, even if it was hard work like stacking wood or piling brush. She also loved to go hunting and fishing with the boys in the family. Tristan would often take her fishing on their grandparents' land when she was a tween.

However, she did not like to openly express her feelings very often. She would retreat to her room or talk to one of her sisters about the things that were bothering her. This was difficult for me at times as her mom, but I was always so grateful they had each other to talk to.

In 2015, Steven was offered a promotion, and we relocated our family from the only life they had known in Bradford, Vermont, to East Longmeadow, Massachusetts. It was a completely different scene for all of us, a more active community, and the kids got involved very quickly with sports and school activities. They really thrived, doing well in school and making a lot of new friends. Sierra and Aspen attended dances and parties and went to Friday night football games at the high school stadium where their older brother, Tristan, played. Life was going well for our family.

However, due to events outside of our control, we were only there for three years and moved back in the fall of 2018. It was a difficult transition for Sierra and Aspen to come back to school as sophomores after leaving in the sixth grade. During the time they lived out of state, their friends had moved on and developed different friend groups with other kids. Sierra and Aspen had also grown and changed.

Steven and I felt the same as the girls. Many of our friends had divorced or were separated. A lot had changed. We were all feeling out of place.

As a family, we had expected to just slot back into the lives we had known for so long, but it was not that easy. It felt like we had been away for a lot longer than three years. Returning to Vermont was a tough transition.

The twins continued their sophomore year at Oxbow High School while Tanner was finishing sixth grade. Although after the initial bumps in the road, after several months of settling back "home," things gradually got easier.

The twins started working at Pierson's farmstand in Bradford in the spring of 2019, and they also enrolled in Driver's Ed in the fall of that year. They both passed in March 2020 and suddenly, we had two new drivers in the family. It was such an exciting time for them as another big step to independence. We purchased both girls safe and reliable secondhand cars: an Audi Q5 for Aspen and a BMW X5 for Sierra. Both vehicles were almost as old as the girls.

They loved their cars! Sierra especially loved hers; she would wash it, clean the windows, and vacuum it weekly. It did not have the technology of vehicles today, and it was well used prior to purchasing it, but to Sierra, it was perfect! She liked that it was so unique. Little did we know that buying that car would play a key role in protecting her. The car was a metal tank made in Germany.

As time went on, familiar routines continued to reconnect us to the area in which our kids had grown up. Life was good. I started my own business in the summer of 2019, a business I could grow substantially. After the initial bumpy readjustment, everyone seemed happy and content that we moved back, especially Steven's family, whom we had not seen very often in the three years while we were away. The kids were also happy to be back closer to their Grandparents.

In September 2019, Sierra met a boy who was a year older than her at school. They appeared to get along well and were together a lot. She was elated, her energy contagious as they started dating. She was infatuated with him; he was totally different from anyone else she had been interested in before. They were always texting and calling each other, often dozens of times a day. From the outside, it seemed sweet, and we were initially happy for her. However, as the days turned to weeks, we started to notice things change.

My husband and I are understandably protective of our children, and we pay attention as the character of our children's partners begins to unfold. This boy was pompous and sarcastic and did not make a good first (or second or third) impression on us. Nonetheless, we gave him the benefit of the doubt. Steven and I decided to support Sierra in her decision because she seemed happy (at first), and she was our fiercely responsible girl. We did not even consider the possibility that she could be manipulated into a romantic relationship. After all, they were just teenagers.

A few months after they started dating, Aspen told us about behavior she had witnessed from this boy towards Sierra. Aspen thought something seemed off to her, like he was trying to control her, both physically and mentally. Just a slight push here, or grabbing her arm there, or sarcastically telling her she was an idiot in front of others and then laughing it off like it was a joke.

Saying demeaning things became normal, and he would never apologize, only expecting apologies from Sierra. We learned that he would encourage her to do things he knew were not moral and then chastise her for it. He continually played mind games with her, making her doubt herself, which was something she was not accustomed to or knew how to deal with.

When we asked Sierra about these incidents, she emphatically denied them happening and said she could handle whatever came her way. We trusted her because we knew what a strong-willed, smart young lady we had raised. It wasn't until after the crash that we learned the full extent of the abuse she was hiding and coping with on her own.

A few weeks after the conversation with Aspen, I attended a dinner with a few moms from the high school booster club. During casual conversation, I heard stories about Sierra's new boyfriend. Unbeknownst to us, he had a reputation for fighting, being suspended, and reckless driving. I was immediately concerned for Sierra's safety when I came home that night. I shared what I had been told with Steven. We talked with Sierra about the things I had heard. She seemed surprised and agreed to talk to him about it.

When she questioned her boyfriend, he dismissed every accusation against him. Sure, those things happened, but none of it was his fault. He was in the wrong place at the wrong time; someone else pushed him into it, and someone else started it. He just had bad luck. Someone had a grudge against him. People were just out to get him. He was innocent.

We weren't convinced, but Sierra believed in him and whatever he told her. We didn't know that he had started using her as a punching bag, and she thought it was somehow her fault and that he didn't really understand that it was wrong. She let it go on and did her best not to provoke him, thinking that it was just the unspoken parts of being in a relationship.

Over the following weeks, Sierra's personality started to change. Her grades were dropping, she lost interest in the sports she had previously loved and played year-round, her physical appearance changed, she lost pounds and became very thin, and she was very irritable around her family.

Previously happy to play a game or hang out with Tanner, her younger brother, now she was not interested in spending any time with him and would yell at him to leave her alone or get out of her room. She was always in her room, choosing not to be involved with the friendly family chat around dinnertime. She would come out to eat and immediately go back to her solitude. Any attempts to involve her were rebuffed. It was difficult to watch. Whenever any of us tried to talk to her, she would assure us that things were fine, that he treated her well, and that she loved him.

After witnessing these fundamental and alarming changes in our daughter's personality for a few months, we decided in June 2020 that enough was enough, and they needed to have some space. We thought that Sierra could do with a change of perspective by not being around him all the time. We reached out to her boyfriend's mother to let her know that her son and our daughter needed to take a break. He was no longer welcome at our house; she was not to go to his house, and they could only see each other in public.

On July 3, Sierra went out with her sister, Lindsay, to hang out with her and her friends at a bonfire. Lindsay and Sierra have always been relatively close; they share the same compassionate and caring outlook, but while Sierra is quiet and shy, Lindsay is not.

Sierra had always looked up to Lindsay, and Lindsay recognized some unhealthy signs in her younger sister's relationship, which she spoke to her about. Sierra opened up a little and told Lindsay how controlling he had become. She was ashamed to tell anyone, feeling like it was her fault and that she had failed as a girlfriend.

At Lindsay's insistence, Sierra turned her phone's shared location off, which she had been fearful of doing as he told her to always make sure it was on so he knew where she was. Because he loved her and wanted to know she was safe.

At the bonfire, a girl who had dated the boyfriend before Sierra approached Lindsay and told her he had been cheating with her and showed Lindsay explicit text messages, provocative photos, and phone records he had sent her. Lindsay, of course, told Sierra, and with Lindsay's encouragement, Sierra decided she had had enough. It was not healthy, and it was time to end the relationship.

On July 4th, Sierra gathered his belongings, drove to his house, and told him it was over. She did not want to see him anymore. Steven and I decided to follow her to make sure she was safe.

He then spent the next three days blowing up her phone with texts and phone calls that went from trying to convince her to take him back to blaming everyone else and telling her she was wrong to outright threats of retribution. We did not know any of this until we looked through her phone after the crash, trying to figure out what happened that morning. At that time, we still had so many questions: how had this happened? Had she been texting? Why was she speeding? We felt there was so much more to the crash than the initial findings.

Steven and I were grateful things were over between them. The timing was perfect, as we were about to go on our family vacation, and Sierra could move forward in her life without his controlling behavior (we did not know about the violence at the time). She was also excited to hang out with one of her older brother's friends who would be there and whom she had a crush on. We were ready to put it all behind us.

She and Aspen were going to enjoy their summer before their senior year of high school; we were sure things would start to level out for her from then on.

The whole relationship had lasted less than a year. Yet he had managed to get into her head and instill the thought that she should believe everything he said, that he loved her more than anyone else ever would. Nobody else would ever love her. That everything he did to her was her fault. Without him, she was nothing.

We couldn't understand how Sierra had succumbed to such controlling behavior and abuse. There was nobody in her family, friend group, or church community in abusive relationships, so I started taking notice of the other important influences, especially that of romance and relationships in movies and TV shows.

Often starting with the viewing targeted at tweens, this made me realize that the line between romantic and unhealthy relationship behaviors is blurry. Too often in romantic TV and film roles, jealousy is mistaken for caring and possessiveness is confused with power, co-dependence is portrayed as sweet, and when these well-known couples become beloved within pop culture, thanks to the compelling and beautiful actors who play them, it normalizes these examples for impressionable viewers, especially teens and young adults.

Sierra told me later that she had not been familiar with real relationship stuff before this relationship, only the little kid stuff she had experienced before. She had mistakenly presumed that emotional manipulation and violence were just something normal that some people experienced at some point in relationships.

Looking back, it was such stereotypical narcissistic behavior on his part; I was shocked that it wasn't even on our radar as parents. We had never experienced such behavior in someone connected to our family before. And as a result, we were as blindsided by it as Sierra was.

Even though she had also participated in a program when we lived in East Longmeadow called "UnifyAgainst Bullying," she did not recognize how easily she had succumbed to it once we returned to Vermont. She was ashamed to tell anyone what was going on because of her own close-knit family and upbringing. He had effectively isolated her.

I realized that even though Steven and I modeled healthy boundaries, respect, and communication in our relationship. We had never openly discussed with the children the toxic traits and different mindsets and beliefs other kids are brought up with concerning respect and relationships. I have noticed more and more often in society, the toxicity modeled on television and in film seems to be the only role models a lot of kids have.

We have since started discussing these things within our family, asking their opinions on what they see depicted on film and television as well as social media. Reminding them that those things are only there for entertainment and are not real.

Hopefully, they will have the courage to talk about those ideas or recognize when that is happening to one of their friends, too. So often, the person subjected to such behavior is ashamed and doesn't know how to tell anyone. They don't even feel like they can tell their friends.

Bullying and abuse, especially among teens, are a silent and invisible issue in our communities. We hope to be able to start conversations in places where it has been ignored for way too long.

Chapter Nine – Spiritual Revelations

⁶ Be strong and of good courage, do not fear nor be afraid of them; for the LORD your God, He *is* the One who goes with you. He will not leave you nor forsake you." Deuteronomy 31:6

As the days turned into weeks, Sierra continued to progress, relearning the basics of being able to have as much independence as she could. She was becoming more confident in herself as the weeks went on; some weeks, she made massive physical progress; other weeks, it was her emotional maturity that evolved, and we started having some revealing conversations with her about what she experienced while she was in the medically induced coma.

We knew she had been there, suspended between life and death. We knew the power of prayer had offered a huge source of comfort for our family, but we had not fully comprehended the impact it had on her and what she felt and saw or the conversations she had with people no longer on this plane.

If someone had suggested to me even six months beforehand that any of this was possible, I wouldn't have been surprised but may have been a little skeptical. Although we are very spiritual people and open to the metaphysical, it would have been difficult to understand the volume of blessings Sierra experienced.

We believe in the power of God, and as we had already experienced so many miracles on Sierra's journey, it all made perfect sense. After everything we had experienced, I had stopped looking through critical eyes months ago. I now viewed things through my heart first. And my heart knew Sierra had received a divine intervention.

Little by little, as she grew more confident in her communication, she shared with us the people she had seen and the things she was told while in a coma. As we heard her story, we were continually humbled by the events that transpired to bring Sierra back to us. She was very hesitant to share many of the details. However, it almost seemed like she did not think we were ready to hear what she had been told.

Often, she would even say, "I'm not sure I am supposed to tell you this."

Being a faith-filled family, this was powerful to us, but little did we know the extent of what it meant. But overall, she was eager to share her experiences with us.

Right from the time of the crash, Sierra had memories of being outside of her body. Almost as soon as she had been moved to the hospital room, she remembers leaving her injured body and feeling extremely worried and concerned, wanting to check on us. She was unsure what had happened to her or where she was, but she knew it was bad.

First, she went to Aspen, as she could feel her twin so distraught and inconsolable, and she saw Aspen and her boyfriend in the room together, praying for her to return. Much later, when Sierra and Aspen spoke about her visit, Sierra remembered the details of the room that she had never physically been in.

There was a table and a couch where Aspen and her boyfriend had been sitting, but most unusually, she remembered the kitchenette and stackable washer and dryer in the corner of the room. Aspen was amazed to realize it was exactly when her boyfriend had said he felt an angel in the room with them and when she had felt a sense of peace overwhelm her.

The next people she went to were Steven and I. She was so worried about us. She said she could also feel our concern for her as she tried to break through, first by speaking to us, and then as she realized we could not hear her, she tried yelling and screaming that she was okay.

One night, Steven woke up to the sound of Sierra whispering in his ear. He was sure it was her.

She said, "Dad, I'm okay."

Steven felt a breeze in his ear as is someone had whispered very closely. Later, we realized it had been her screaming, still trying to get his attention. It was incredibly frustrating for her because it felt like she could just speak to us. She thought we couldn't hear her and did not know she was there. She perceived that Steven and I were heartbroken at the thought of never hearing her voice again, which was unlike any pain I had ever experienced.

From where she was in the spiritual realm, Sierra could read the hearts of her family, and she knew we were all devastated by what had happened to her. This, of course, upset her too because she did not know how to break through to communicate with us. Or if she would ever be able to again.

Just before her crash, Sierra had been feeling lost and separated from the devout Catholic upbringing she was raised with. After experiencing an abusive relationship with her ex, she had been struggling with her faith. And although she wanted to believe, she just couldn't connect to God's presence the way she once had.

Steven and I had not realized she had been feeling that way, more concerned with having the influence of her boyfriend out of our home. We had not thought to talk to her about her faith. But once she was able to start communicating with us about these things, we were blown away.

After showing her the items from her shrine and sharing with me in Spaulding that she had seen the younger version of Padre Pio while she was in a coma at Dartmouth, I wondered if she had seen anyone else. She spoke as if it was the most normal conversation. Our family often talked about how St. Padre Pio entered our lives as well.

The patron saint of miracles and healing had made his presence known in such a wonderful, supportive way in all our lives at about the same time. We talked often about how it was divine timing and surely not a coincidence. One of Steven's favorite sayings is, "there are no coincidences," and as time went on, the more I agreed with this sentiment.

I was dying to ask Sierra more questions about his visit, as there were so many things I wanted to know. Although, even with all my curiosity, I didn't ask her. She was already going through so much that I knew she would tell us as she remembered and felt ready to share.

The next time she mentioned her memories of being in a coma, she went further into detail about that visitation with St. Padre Pio. He was the first person she saw. It is no coincidence that he was also introduced to me through a complete stranger early on. A young man with dark hair wearing a brown cloak, she clearly remembered thinking, "Where am I? What is happening?"

She felt scared and uneasy. When she saw him, she did not understand the context or why she was there, in that place. Like how she felt when she first left her body, she just felt anxious about who this person was and why he was there.

Right up until I had shown her the prayer card with his more mature likeness on it, Sierra had been unsure who the visitor was. But she remembered his visit in vivid detail: the background was white, and the focus was only on him as he approached her.

As he looked at her, she felt he was looking deep into her soul. His presence and demeanor were calming and comforting. Sierra felt the anxiety leave her body.

She knew she was safe, and he told her, "You are going to be okay; your family is waiting for you when you wake up."

Sierra did not answer him because she was confused as to why he was telling her this, but she remembered the peaceful feeling she felt from his words. She didn't hear his voice; the communication was telepathic, and his words were spoken directly in her mind. As she gazed at him, curious about who he was, she felt everything would be ok. She blinked, and he was gone. The feelings instilled by him remained, though, and she became more curious than anxious.

After she shared with us the details of St. Padre Pio's visit, we told Sierra about how we connected with him, too, and she wanted to go to the St. Padre Pio Center in Pennsylvania. Right then, we decided we would make an annual pilgrimage when she was healthy enough to travel.

Sierra told us she had been visited by three people while she was in a medically induced coma. It was some time until she mentioned the other visitors she had, but I was comforted by hearing about her next visitor. It was my mother, her grandmother, in a younger form. I can only imagine that on the other side, people are represented by their healthiest incarnation, usually in their 20s and 30s—sometimes younger.

I felt so relieved that my mom had been there for her. But I was not surprised; my mother was a very caring and loving person who doted on her whole family, especially her grandchildren, so the fact that she still looked out for my children from the spiritual realm felt reassuring. And after the experience at Dartmouth in the chapel, when the scent of her perfume was all around me as I had reentered Sierra's room that night in July, it made sense that she had been there for us all. Still giving her love and support from the heavenly realm.

At the time of the crash, my mother had been gone for almost six years. The last time the girls had seen her, they were just twelve years old. Although she had lived in Buffalo, New York, she was a very influential figure in my children's lives. The distance did not prevent her from having close relationships with all her grandchildren.

When Sierra was approached by her grandmother, she too was much younger, around Sierra's own age, and even though at first Sierra did not realize who she was, she quickly recognized her beloved grandmother's energy and felt relieved and comforted by her presence. She did not speak to Sierra but radiated comfort through their connection.

They exchanged such depth of feeling that words were not necessary. Sierra said the feeling of love filled more than just her heart. It felt like a warm glow emanating from her grandmother directly into her heart, mind, and soul.

The third person who visited her was someone Sierra had seen a lot of pictures of growing up. Even though she knows everyone has their own beliefs about Jesus and his appearance, she knew this was Him.

This visit was different from the rest. It was extra vivid and defined. She was still in the all-white environment when she saw a human form outlined by a blinding bright white light that was moving towards her. The light emanated peace and love. She felt as though she was in the presence of God. She felt drawn towards it. As the human form drew closer to her from the white light, He came into sharp focus, and she became unaware of the background, that it just kind of faded away.

He, too, was wearing a brown cloak, although He had light brown hair, a short beard, and intensely bright, beautiful ice blue eyes. She will never forget His eyes. He was looking at her very intently. Again, she felt a similar feeling she had experienced with the first visitor like he was staring into her heart and soul, that He could see all of her.

He came closer so they were face to face and put his hand on her shoulder, which felt warm and electric like His hand was vibrating with pure energy, and a deep, almost indescribable feeling of powerful, all-encompassing love swept through her like a wave of warmth and fullness. She had no doubts about his identity. She knew immediately from his powerful presence it was Jesus himself.

He looked at her kindly and said, "Everything is going to be OK; you only have one choice to make."

At first, Sierra was unsure what the choice was.

Looking at him unsure, He continued, "Do you want to go back to your family?"

She did not need to be asked twice and nodded vigorously, desperately wanting to return to us. After visiting us and feeling our despair, she fully understood that her place was with her family. She knew that we all missed her so very much and that we wished more than anything that we could trade places, that we all felt broken without her.

At that moment, Sierra's mind was opened to all the things that are so easily taken for granted as we move though life. It did not matter how loving or annoying a family could be to each other. It can all be taken away in a flash. She realized that tomorrow is not always promised, and at any moment, a person can be forced to evaluate their journey and make a choice to rejoin their life or not. She saw that life is a gift and understood that love is the universal language to lift and unify us all.

Sierra knew her life was not finished yet, that she must return to share the story of her journey and, most importantly, to the love of her family. She knew God had a bigger plan for her.

We were not surprised when she told us this. By the time she was healed enough to tell us what she had experienced, the number of people who reached out, who followed Sierra's story and got involved and came together, showed us that God was already using her and her journey in ways we did not fully comprehend.

We knew Sierra had been blessed with a miracle but had not realized the extent until she shared the full visitation stories with us. Knowing how blessed she was, we shared the news with our priest, Father Andrew, who requested permission to share the story with the local religious community.

In December 2020, the Roman Catholic Diocese of Burlington magazine featured an article on Sierra's journey, which mentioned the support we received from our home church, Our Lady of Perpetual Help, where the parishioners had started a rosary prayer chain and continued to pray for Sierra. The article also mentioned the visitations she experienced with St. Padre Pio and God and the observation that Sierra's experience had brought others back to church. 'The Journey' of Sierra Longmoore

It wasn't until sometime later that other people came to me and let me know of their experiences around Sierra's injuries as well, especially in those first few days when she was in a coma.

Steven's cousin, Tim, had discovered a few months before the crash that he had metaphysical insight and was regularly experiencing out-of-body astral travel in his sleep. This had obviously come as somewhat of a shock to him, as he was an accountant and had never been interested in those things previously.

As our extended family is very close, he was as devastated as everyone else upon hearing the news of Sierra's crash. He was sure he could find her and communicate with her in the dream state and spent the three nights after the crash praying and asking for assistance to find Sierra.

On Monday morning, he awoke and knew he had found her. That same day, he started experiencing blurred and spiraling vision, which created massive episodes of dizziness and nausea, followed by vomiting and profuse sweating with periods of freezing cold and incredible body tremors where he had no control of his body.

After this continued for a few days, he visited his doctor, who ran extensive tests and scheduled a CT scan where all tests were inconclusive. They settled on a diagnosis of a mysterious neurological disease because nothing else fit.

He was displaying the symptoms of a traumatic brain injury, yet his brain was fine. He knew Sierra had a severe traumatic brain injury and wondered if, somehow, he was picking up on her energetic experiences with it. As the days passed, he was sure he was processing it as well. He spent a lot of time praying and meditating for healing for Sierra and could detect the massive community of support and love directed toward her while she was in the coma.

After a couple of weeks of this, he met a woman at his work who immediately asked what was happening in his life. He told her about the upcoming CT scan and mystery neurological diagnosis (feeling too self-conscious to speak of his real thoughts on the matter or of Sierra's injury.)

The woman nodded and asked if he knew someone with a TBI. After he said that he did, she explained to him that he had taken on the energy of a serious head injury from somebody else, which was why he was experiencing all those symptoms. She also told him about the details of his past life, visions he had experienced, and the spirits and guides he had been working with.

She gave him great clarity on many things he did not understand himself. This also bought him great peace, as it made sense. He continued praying and meditating daily for Sierra's recovery, and as she awoke from the coma, his symptoms disappeared.

He was not the only person to communicate that they had had an experience with Sierra's injury.

Gretchen is a Certified Personal Trainer and Fitness Nutritionist turned Transformation Specialist.

Transformation Specialists are trained in the skills and techniques required to coach and influence behavioral patterns as they relate to the client, and I reached out to her in July 2021 to work with Sierra. It was not until she had been working with Sierra for a few more months that she shared her own experience in the days after Sierra's crash. Gretchen had been aware of a groundswell of support for Sierra with all the #Sierrastrong signage and t-shirts, etc.

Her son worked at the bank with Steven's mother, and he had been part of the campaign to raise money for her, but she did not personally know our family. She had also been on her own metaphysical journey in search of a diagnosis for her son, who remained undiagnosed with a muscle degeneration condition.

Experiencing and feeling things had started to become common place for Gretchen, so she was not too surprised when her first vision occurred on the morning of the crash. She was driving one afternoon when she saw a teenaged girl having a face-to-face meeting with God himself. She was aware of massive amounts of energy passing between them, and then the girl smiled and nodded as she closed her eyes and raised her chin.

She was enveloped in a brilliant, all-encompassing light as the vision dissipated, and at the same time, Gretchen heard, "She has chosen. Sierra is coming back."

Gretchen knew it must be the same Sierra and momentarily thought about trying to contact us to tell us what she saw. She knew Sierra would make a full recovery. But she also knew that we had a lot of support, and she did not know how to pass that information along without seeming like a random crazy person.

A little later, she saw a mutual acquaintance who she knew believed in metaphysical and shared with her that she had seen Sierra's meeting with God and that she would be making a full recovery. Our friend was excited to hear that, as it was what we were all praying for.

Gretchen also knew one day, she would be working with Sierra and felt that Sierra and our family were very definitely being held and protected by divine power.

By this time, our family's mindset had been permanently altered. Nothing surprised us anymore. We had all seen and felt too many things that defied logical explanation. It all just served to strengthen our faith in the Lord Almighty as the ruler of everything. We knew that having brought us this far, His continual signs and symbols just proved He would not be deserting us now.

Chapter Ten – Our Orange Family

[2] Bear one another's burdens, and so fulfill the law of Christ.

Galatians 6:2

By 2020, Steven had been working for Home Depot for a little over twenty-three years in the New England area. At the time of Sierra's crash, he had been a District Manager for six years, which meant he was responsible for ten Home Depot Stores throughout the New England region.

Having the perspective of working his way through the positions from where he started as a frontline associate gives him a unique perspective and empathy for his staff, and he is respected by everyone he works with and for.

The overall Home Depot culture, mindset, and values of building strong relationships based on trust and honesty, along with respecting and taking care of people as well as doing the right thing, resonates deeply with our family and has bonded dozens of management offices and many frontline staff.

At some point, almost all members of our family have been part of the Home Depot community, either working part-time or full-time, for a summer or a few years. The company has been a big part of our lives and for which we are incredibly grateful.

I personally was touched by the many interviews and testimonies shared about Steven's leadership and the impact he has on his people.

Steven takes considerable pride in his people and setting a high standard for them by example. His inclusive attitude is infectious, and he chooses to see the best in everyone, encouraging their strengths and empowering them to be the best people they can be.

His leadership provides a solid foundation for many people to look up to and model themselves on. This became apparent and was especially humbling as news of Sierra's crash spread throughout the Home Depot organization.

Right from those first dark days of uncertainty as word spread, the outpouring of support from the Home Depot family (HD Family) seemed to come from every direction. All were incredibly encouraging, leaping into action, sending us pictures, gifts, food, and messages of support in mere hours as the news spread. From frontline associates to the CEO and vice president, other managers, and distribution centers, the support was like a giant soft blanket wrapping around our family.

Christina Roberts was the Operations Manager in Westfield, Massachusetts, and she was promoted by Steven shortly after our relocation to East Longmeadow. He had been a valuable mentor for her, building her confidence through professional support and development.

She had four children herself, similar in age to our own, and they would share stories of the kids' accomplishments. We often attended the same sports events and took pride in each other's family's achievements.

When she heard of the crash, even though she had been on vacation, she quickly rallied her store management, associates, and staff to send messages of support and gifts to us. They made posters and videos, sent messages of powerful encouragement, and tweeted them continuously. She and her team sent us the angel light to watch over Sierra, which was one of the first items on her shrine.

In the days immediately after the crash, the #SierraStrong phrase was developed by the HD Family, and the bracelets were first made and sold through the Home Depot staff, with all proceeds coming back to our family. The outpouring of support was incredible to witness, and in the first week, as updates were being sent to the New England stores, they rapidly spread to other stores through social media.

Jessica Meaney was the store manager in Wilbraham, Massachusetts, and she organized her nine store manager peers and district team leaders to take a trip to Boston to sit outside Spaulding, where they could be seen from Sierra's window with banners and balloons to show their support for Sierra and our family. Due to COVID-19 visitor restrictions, they could not enter the building, but the love and support sent from afar were emotional and touching.

We were often brought to tears with the thoughtfulness and generosity of spirit shown by her team. Her unwavering dedication in supporting our family at this time was a testament to her personal strength as well as The Home Depot's community spirit and Steven's effect on his teams.

Many of the New England associates had been with The Home Depot for years and were familiar with our children and the twins especially. Quite a few of them have very fond memories of the girls running around at various Home Depot events or when I stopped by the store for whatever reason when they were younger.

Steven is a very proud dad and has always been generous with details of all our children's sports and academic achievements with his teams at work. This has bonded many of his employees and coworkers with our family, who vicariously rooted for our kids' teams and achievements, so when the news of Sierra's crash was first shared, many of the associates were grief-stricken that such a tragic event had occurred to one of their own. We received many voice messages of support and people letting us know they were praying or going back to church and getting reacquainted with their faith to request a miracle for Sierra.

Steven had become friends with Jason Arigoni, the Vice President of The Home Depot. Before he was based in Atlanta, Jason had begun his tenure in the New England area, where Steven had gone above and beyond to make "the new guy" feel welcome.

The previous VP had been with The Home Depot for an exceptionally long time and was the only one Steven knew during his career up until that point. It was only natural for him to reach out to assist the new VP in any way he could to show him the ropes.

They quickly developed a mutual respect and personal friendship and would text each other often, sharing stories about family along with a friendly football rivalry. After the crash, Jason personally would check in with Steven regularly and then relay the information about Sierra's condition to the rest of The Home Depot community. This was a wonderful relief.

Although we were grateful for all the concern of others wanting to be kept updated on Sierra's condition, it was beyond our emotional capability to keep communication open with dozens of people. So, having a couple of trusted others sharing the information and difficulties of our journey certainly lightened the load. The Miracle for Sierra Facebook page was another straightforward way to keep people in touch with Sierra's journey.

After the first week of being at Dartmouth, 24/7 realism set in, and Steven started to worry about his work responsibilities and how he would return. This was quickly laid to rest as his peers stepped up to cover his work area and ensured he did not have to worry about anything besides being available for his family and Sierra.

The Home Depot mindset of success and positivity in the workplace by taking care of the family was being reflected in us, and it was incredible. Word spread very quickly, and it seemed within no time at all, the messages of support that had been regional came flooding in from the entire country. This wave of love and support was also very uplifting.

As Steven kept Jason updated on Sierra's condition, Steven knew his place was with Sierra and his family and had voiced his concerns about leaving for an indefinite period. Jason understood, and although he had already coordinated multiple leaders to cover the district for a few weeks, which had worked well as a stopgap measure, it was time to have a more stable presence in the temporary position.

A Territory Operations Manager named Rosa Dyer covered for multiple weeks, and Steven was given an extended leave of three months. The team wanted to make the goals for his home store, not wanting him to worry about falling behind at work while he had so much else going on, and he managed to exceed goals for the quarter.

Steven had built friendships over the years with other corporate associates, too. And, although they had all been so uplifting for us, we had not realized until much later how much we had impacted them, too.

John Carr, the Regional Director of Merchandizing, had an overwhelming urge to call Steven one day about three weeks after the crash, and they spoke at length. Being the first time Steven had really gotten to share his perspective and feelings with a trusted friend, this hour-long conversation had a cathartic effect on Steven and had a huge impact on John's own life.

He was inspired by our family's devotion and dedication to Sierra and each other, which in turn made him look at his family with new eyes. From that day, he understood that family really is the most important thing, and although work is important, it is family that deserves our focus.

This had a noticeable ripple effect through many stores and associates, too, inspired by our family's strength and faith, our way of sticking together through it all and praying for a miracle. Little did we know at the time, but our family became as much of an inspiration for so many within the HD family as they were for us.

A month after the crash, many Home Depots hosted a #SierraStrong day where many of the 500,000 associates from across the U.S. joined in, showing their love and support through various actions and events. They made it a huge day.

They sold t-shirts and bracelets, and there were bucket challenges, food, and fun throughout all the stores. This brought so many people together in such a positive way, which had been lacking due to all the uncertainty from COVID-19 and all the restrictions. They all fully embraced this incredible cause for Sierra and our family.

As time passed, each update was eagerly received by the associates who were so invested in Sierra's recovery. It felt like the whole company was pulling for her. When Sierra was starting to speak again, Steven and Sierra facetimed with Jason, which was incredibly inspiring for him. Jason later told us he felt blessed to have witnessed what a miracle Sierra had been through to get to that point.

He knew Sierra was going to be different and face continual challenges from such a life-altering event, but he did not expect to see such changes in Steven, who was well-known for his stoic presence and grit. Jason also observed a ripple effect of deeper gratitude and positivity from our family's unwavering faith, offering inspiration to all management and board members he interacted with by appreciating the time they had with their loved ones and each other so much more.

Once Steven returned to work, there was a noticeable change in the way he counseled his peers, offering a strong faith-based, family approach, which was welcomed and appreciated. Previously, he had been hesitant to share the depth of his faith and belief in God and the church out of respect for others' beliefs. And even though they never felt he had been withholding anything about himself, he is noticeably more open and more readily available to offer his faith-based assistance.

After witnessing the effects of prayer and God granting miracles to his own daughter, he could not withhold that part of himself any longer.

This became obvious three months later. When he returned to work, there were several incidents with his associates, from a late-term pregnancy loss to the unexpected death of a coworker. All shocking events and the team needed a lot of support, which Steven selflessly offered, becoming a pillar of strength for them all in challenging times.

In December 2020, Steven was asked to write a piece for the Culture Spotlight in the HD Orange quarterly magazine that is sent to all staff and associates. Culture Spotlight is a team member relating a story or recent event from their lives.

Sometimes it's an accomplishment, sometimes sharing a wonderful or not-so-wonderful life event. It is an effective way to share stories with the entire HD Family. Steven felt good that he had the opportunity to thank everyone for their actions and prayers and that it had not gone unnoticed.

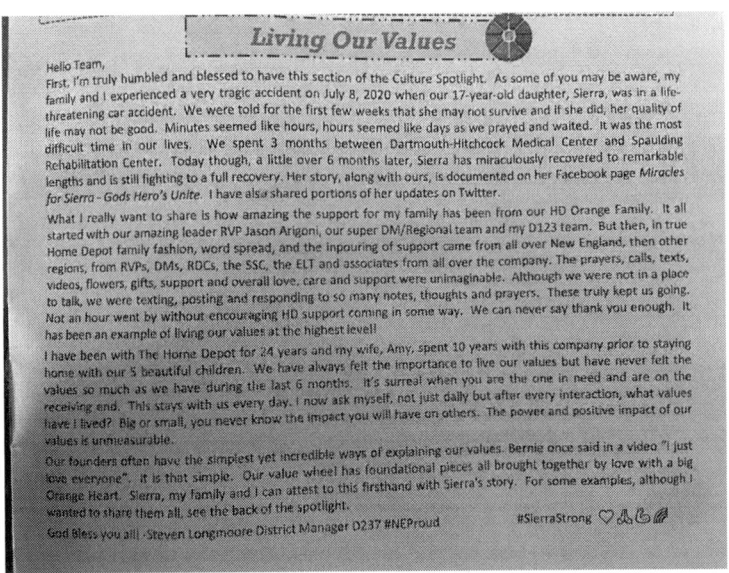

All we ever asked for from anyone was prayers, and we have been amazed in the time since, the number of people from The Home Depot family that have told us that Sierra's crash was the sole reason they revisited their own churches, which they had drifted away from during COVID-19.

To realize that many associates who were of differing faiths or had not been in a church for years started praying again or went back to church and places of worship for Sierra made us start to realize that we were part of a bigger faith walk in every area of our lives.

As time has passed, we have come to understand that it was not just what The Home Depot family did for us during 2020 and beyond but what we also did for them in the process, exemplifying family love and unbreakable bonds and the power of pulling together as one cohesive unit. The importance of putting family first was a takeaway that many have told us has stuck with them since then.

Chapter Eleven - Milestones

¹⁷ The LORD your God in your midst,
The Mighty One, will save;
He will rejoice over you with gladness,
He will quiet *you* with His love,
He will rejoice over you with singing." Zephaniah 3:17

As we got further into October, our family was excited for a Halloween family wedding, which had been years in the planning and one we had been looking forward to since it was announced in 2019. We had discussed costumes and a family theme for months until Sierra's crash. Then, it became the last thing on our minds.

We did not want to speculate that we might not be able to attend. Right up until we returned home with Sierra, we were unsure if we would be going. Sierra, however, was adamant she would be able to attend, and our family planned accordingly.

Sierra was also very excited as Tristan's friend, Hayden, was also going to be there (this was the friend she had a crush on and was looking forward to spending some time with on the camping trip we didn't make back in July). This extra motivation really accelerated her progress, and again, she amazed us all with the dedication and focus she showed in her therapies leading up to the event.

Our family picked a DC comics theme: Steven was the Joker, I was Poison Ivy, Grandpa Steve was Batman, and Sierra went as Harley Quinn. She was so happy to be doing something normal again. As part of a large extended family, we have numerous family parties and gatherings throughout the year, so it felt good to have a moment of familiarity and celebration in our now permanently altered lives.

Hayden and Tristan had been friends for years, and he knew our family and Sierra's story well. That evening, he was such a gentleman, knowing how Sierra felt about him and what she had been through. They talked and danced for hours. He made her feel special without pretense. He was as happy to see her at the wedding as she was to be there.

I was so happy for her, as another milestone had been reached. As she gained coherency in her memories and watched Aspen, Sierra knew she was missing the social aspect of her senior year of high school, and this event eased some of that for her. This was also a huge motivator, and she kept working hard in all her therapies to make up for lost time.

In November 2020, we made our first trip as a family to the National Center for Padre Pio in Barto, Pennsylvania. It was a beautiful fall day in Pennsylvania, and we walked the grounds in the afternoon sunshine. There was such a beautiful energy that seemed to emanate from the entire center and outdoor areas.

We walked around the church, the chapel, the museum, and the gift shop. We toured the museum, which had many artifacts of Padre Pios' life. There were also many photos detailing the timeline of his life and the graces he received from the Lord. There was also a small theatre that featured a twenty-minute video of Padre Pio's life. As we watched, Sierra and I were amazed as the picture I had shown her in Spaulding after she talked about his visit was featured often in the film. She was excited. It was like she saw an old friend.

As we moved around the complex, we ended up in the gift shop, where we purchased a few items to commemorate our first visit to the center. The lady behind the counter asked where we were from. I briefly told her about Sierra's journey and why we had come. A few of the other customers heard what I said and asked to touch Sierra as she had been touched by Padre Pio.

Within a few minutes, she was swarmed by a tour bus of people who were shopping as well, excited to interact with someone who had been visited by Padre Pio. This was very overwhelming, and all the attention was too much for Sierra, triggering an anxiety attack. Aspen hastily but politely shuffled her out of the shop and back to the serenity of the chapel.

Sierra took some time to breathe and gather herself, and after Aspen checked that the bus had left, we made our way out. Sierra was still relearning so many things, including how to deal with the feeling of being overwhelmed. Overall, though, it was a fulfilling visit, and we affirmed our promise as a family to make an annual pilgrimage to the center.

After we had made the trip to the Padre Pio Center in PA, Sierra continued with her therapies and started talking about graduating high school. Although she was not in any shape to physically go back to school, she really wanted to be able to graduate with her class the following June.

Before the crash, Sierra had hoped to follow in Lindsay's footsteps and go to college to get her nursing degree. She had taken AP classes as a junior to earn college credits, which ended up being helpful in her quest to graduate high school.

She still needed class credits in social studies and English to be able to graduate. As we weighed our options and word spread, one of the high school English teachers reached out to us and offered to tutor Sierra. She had never been taught by this teacher before, but her younger brother Tanner had, and he had enjoyed the time in her classroom.

During the year she taught him, we heard her name often. After meeting with her, we decided she would be a good fit to tutor Sierra. We were also aware that it takes a remarkable individual to volunteer to tutor someone with a TBI.

Sierra met with Ms. Leddy weekly, and she was very patient and kind with her, understanding Sierra's capabilities and structuring the lessons accordingly. They developed a mutual respect, and Sierra worked hard to complete her credit. Once the

English credit had been obtained, Ms. Leddy offered to tutor her for her social studies credit, too. This also went extremely well and had her on track to graduate with her class.

Sierra decided that she wanted to try community college in the Fall of the next year to start working her way toward a degree. She signed up for a pathways program on Early Education through the University of Vermont. Sierra wanted to work with children, as she thought she could have a positive impact on them. Ms. Leddy was a true teacher, invested in her students and encouraging them to reach further, instilling the belief that she could do anything she wanted.

She was certainly a gift in our lives, coming along at exactly the right moment. There was a distinctly different energy in our home that festive season. It was relief and excitement; all of us were so happy to be together as a family.

Thanksgiving 2020 was indeed the most joy-filled and thankful Thanksgiving I can remember. My eldest brother, Vincent, always came from Buffalo, New York, to share the holiday with us, and we had our entire extended family together, which was wonderful. My big brother and I have always been close, and it was quite reassuring for me to have him around for a little while in celebration of our lives.

Having Sierra with us and seeing the miracles performed in her life was beyond anything we felt deserving of as a family, but we were (and still are) so incredibly grateful for God's mercy. It could have quite easily been a different outcome.

Before every meal, we joined together in prayer to bless our food and our guests, with our Thanksgiving meal highlighted, like many other families across the nation, by going around the table and every single one of us saying aloud what we were most grateful for. Thanksgiving 2020 was the year that every member of our family was thankful for Sierra's healing and for our family being present, holding hands, and enjoying the holiday together. Although the Sierra we knew for seventeen years was changed, the new Sierra had threads of familiarity, and she was still an important member of our family.

I understood then that her journey had indeed affected our entire family for the better, altering our own perceptions of what was important in relationships. We were genuinely appreciative of each other and the individual contributions we made to our family group. It was a most beautiful holiday, with each of us being profoundly grateful for the moments we enjoyed together.

The weekend after Thanksgiving, we kept our family tradition of driving to our favorite tree farm in Lyme, New Hampshire, to search for the perfect tree. We searched and searched, taking our time. There was plenty of laughter and joking as we discussed the merits and failures of each person's selection. Finally, we agreed upon the perfect, most beautiful tree for our home. We all took turns with the hacksaw; even Sierra helped, and we triumphantly returned home with our prize.

After all the excitement of Thanksgiving week was done, I drove Sierra to her post-op CAT scan and follow-up from the surgery to reattach her skull just six short weeks before. We did not speak much on the way to the appointment. I was lost in thought and a little worried about the outcome.

We had remained faithful in our prayers and gave thanks to God for every miracle he had bestowed on Sierra to date, but as a mother, I couldn't help but feel worried at times. Her medical team had initially expressed concern about the calcification that had occurred while the piece was gone, but the swelling had gone down very quickly, and she had not experienced any of the expected headaches or migraines in the aftermath, so I was hopeful everything had healed perfectly.

Sierra had the sixty-four staples removed from her head, and the CAT scan was completed. We nervously waited to meet with the doctor to talk about the results, which took an exceptionally long time. I hoped that meant that things were okay, but I felt anxious that they were not.

I reasoned with myself that we would have noticed if she had been declining instead of improving, and she had been improving. In fact, after the initial operation, where she seemed to experience small setbacks, Sierra had been doing extremely well. The doctor who joined us was one of the neurosurgeons who had performed the cranioplasty, and when she came into the room, there was no small talk or trivial pleasantries. She immediately pulled up the two images on her computer.

One was Sierra's brain scan from immediately after the crash, and the CAT scan was taken an hour before. Not only had Sierra's calcified bone reabsorbed with no noticeable side effects, but the fluid had reabsorbed into the brain cavity perfectly.

The parts of her brain that were torn, atrophied, shredded, and barely recognizable within the first twenty-four hours of the crash were healed, and the two scans did not even look like the same brain. There was minimal scar tissue, and everything looked almost normal!

I was as amazed as the doctor, as she kept looking from one image to the other, speechless. The healed brain before us defied explanation. Sierra still had a long road ahead of her, but the difference was incredible. The bleeding, lesions, separated tissue, and destroyed brain matter were simply healed.

Even the doctor was in disbelief and told us that if she did not know any better, she would have presumed that she had pulled up the wrong initial CAT scan. Even she mentioned it looked like a miracle. The doctor encouraged Sierra to keep coming back to visit the medical staff at the hospital because her story gave them a sense of hope.

I could barely hold it together as we left the office. I started crying with joy and disbelief and called Steven as soon as we got back to the car. I could barely speak; I was so excited to share the news and so grateful for the power of God Almighty and his mercy on our family and protection over Sierra. We had certainly been blessed with a miracle. Sierra was more surprised at everyone's reactions than she was at the news her brain had undergone such a miraculous recovery. She said she knew she would be healed.

On the recommendation from the school's director of counseling, we also looked to the school district for support, and Sierra was offered speech and physical therapy through them. Previously accustomed to students with special needs and congenital disabilities, she became the first student in the history of the district to experience a TBI and receive district support.

She was partnered with amazing therapists who worked with her weekly in addition to her outpatient therapies at Dartmouth. Sierra was soaking it all up like a sponge. One of her therapists told me that her positive attitude and determined mindset were such a dream to work with. She was continually inspired to learn more about TBI recovery and develop more intensive sessions for Sierra.

The very next week was my birthday, December 1st, and I was surrounded by love and kindness that year, not just from family but so many messages from afar as well. I was touched by the heartfelt wishes I received from so many people, especially since I had not been a priority even to myself over the course of the previous six months.

One of the most thoughtful gifts I received was from Sierra herself. It was a sketch portrait of my mother. Sierra knew how instrumental my mother had been in my life, that I missed her every single day, and how moved I was when she told me of the visit my mother had made to her while she was in a coma.

The sketch was beautiful, and I treasure it to this day. Amazed that only a few months before, she could not hold any type of writing instrument firmly enough to control it, let alone draw a picture, I was awestruck by the fact that she drew a picture for me.

In the second week of December, we traveled back to Boston to see another vision specialist to have Sierra fitted for glasses. That same day, we also had an appointment at the facial nerve clinic at Massachusetts General Hospital. We checked in at the front desk of the clinic and took a seat in the waiting room. When taking Sierra to her appointments, we never had to wait very long. Any therapy attached to TBI treatments is always on time.

However, this time, we waited for a long time. Her appointment time came and went, and every now and then, I would see clinicians wander in and out of the waiting area as if they were looking for someone or something. Eventually, almost thirty minutes had passed since our appointment time, and I went to the front desk to remind them we were there.

The staff were apologetic and almost embarrassed as they admitted they had been waiting for Sierra to show up in a wheelchair. After reading her medical file and the notes concerning her physical limitations, they assumed she was immobile. I was a little befuddled but mostly amused that, yet again, Sierra had surprised the medical professionals working with her.

From that appointment, Sierra started facial PT once a week. She had to learn how to retrain the muscles in her face to regain movement and control on the left side. Sierra's schedule was full, but she was focused and committed, and the familiar surroundings of home, family, pets, and family gatherings helped make her become cognitively stronger and more confident. As a parent, you often have an intuitive sense of what your child needs to progress, and this was certainly true of Sierra's recovery.

Christmas that year was also a special one, with the girls celebrating their 18th birthday on December 17th. The twin's birthdays occurring a week before Christmas always made for a busy festive season, and this year was no different.

I think my "Miracle for Sierra – God's Heroes Unite" post covered it best:

December 24, 2020.

Day 169: "Sometimes our inability to fix our pain pushes us right into the arms of Jesus."

I have been very sensitive to sharing any initial pictures of Sierra's journey until today, but this one I share with you to put into perspective her miraculous journey to this point.

On the eve of Jesus's birthday, I am reflecting on that July day when a part of our heart and soul was ripped out. So much of our time and effort in this life is consumed by our children's health and well-being. The hopelessness you feel in such a moment is unexplainable.

The quick response of neighbors, first responders, police, fire departments, and DART truly made a positive impact on the outcome of Sierra's survival. I wasn't there on the scene, but God definitely was. His protection that surrounded Sierra shows that God has power over distance and over all things of this physical world.

No one else has that kind of power. He is the only one who can meet our deepest needs in the worst and best of times. Trust Him. #Sierrastrong

"God does not do parlor tricks." ~ CS Lewis

He doesn't perform miracles to impress us. When He performs a miracle, He has a specific purpose in mind beyond the miracle itself.

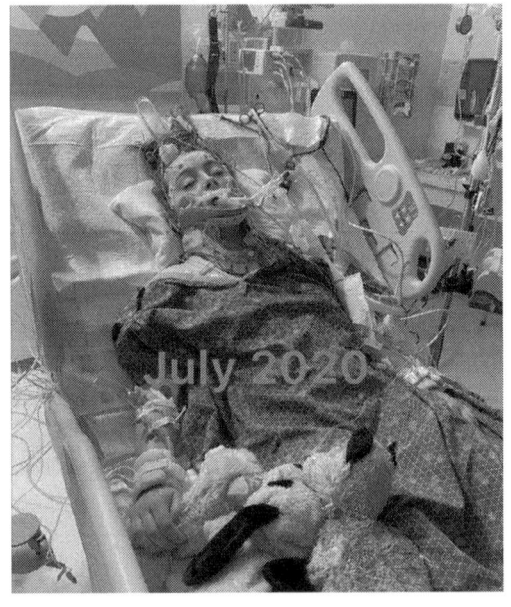

As her self-awareness grew, we wanted to strengthen not only her brain but Sierra's body, too. She was at a point where, besides all the mental and cognitive workouts she was receiving, she was now capable of some physical strengthening, which would help tie her spiritual connections to a stronger base.

In January 2021, still wanting to support local businesses in the area who had reached out and supported us since we returned home, we began working with R.E.P Fitness in Fairlee, Vermont, which was owned by a certified personal trainer, Joey Farley.

I was surprised when I first contacted him in early January about working with her and that he was familiar with her story. He had heard about Sierra's crash through a client near the beginning of August 2020 and had been following Sierra's journey from the beginning.

As a twin himself, he found himself compelled to keep following the updates on the Facebook page and had been celebrating her wins and milestones as she went along, experiencing miraculous moments of recovery. He had even had "We Are Sierra Strong" painted on his gym windows long before we started working with him, wanting to share her inspiring story to inspire others as well.

In that initial conversation, we discussed her potential limitations and set a consultation appointment for a week later. This was to determine where she was at and where they should start. Joey was amazed at how far she had already come with her therapies and could not wait to meet her. He realized that the plan for her would need to be continually evaluated as she progressed.

The moment we walked in the door, I was struck by his genuine nature and sincerity. By this point, we had met dozens of therapists, and while they were all great at what they did, Sierra did not connect with many of them. Very few broke through her introverted and shy exterior; Joey was different.

He wanted her to feel like a regular client, and he engaged her the same way as he did with all his clients who came to him for training. He and Sierra clicked instantly; his care and kindness shone through, making her feel comfortable and capable. They also shared a similar sense of humor and quickly formed a big brother/little sister relationship with sarcastic remarks, good-natured jabs, and realistic challenges.

This was exactly what Sierra needed. Their workouts quickly progressed as her confidence grew, starting with simple exercises and rapidly progressing to more challenging combinations. He seemed to have an intuitive sense of what Sierra needed to get to the next level. She even set a new gym record for the most weight held in a plank position.

Joey and Sierra became good friends. Joey would attend Sierra's softball games and support fundraisers that were important to Sierra. He put a lot into developing her workouts and investigating new exercises that would complement her other therapies.

Seeing how well Sierra was doing with softball, he decided to start some balance training as well, integrating squats on the BOSU ball (the piece of gym equipment that looks like a balance ball cut in half). Sierra completed them the first time with no issue.

She was so overjoyed when she was done that she stepped off the ball, gave Joey a big hug, and said, "Thank you for helping me."

Joey was also so proud of her; he was fighting back tears. Sierra made remarkable strides working with Joey, amazing herself and him.

At the end of January, Sierra was also gifted a scholarship to use the Upper Valley Aquatic Center, which was perfect for keeping up with her new goals. Despite the counseling, Sierra still had moments of intense anxiety and brain fog.

Taking medication helped but did not alleviate the emotional fog she experienced. She was offered a grant for receiving acupuncture. I was not familiar with alternative treatments such as traditional Chinese medicine, but we had heard many positive things about it from lots of people. We thought it was worth a try, and we were so glad we did!

The needles were put in Sierra's ears for 20-30 minutes at a time to stimulate various meridian lines and realign her energy. And to our delight, within a few sessions, we started to notice it working! Sierra was able to calm some of her anxiety and detach from the fog she could not shake until then.

Chapter Twelve – Transformational Strength

[25] Strength and honor *are* her clothing;
She shall rejoice in time to come. Proverbs 31:25

As 2021 unfolded, Sierra still grew stronger. Every week, she was accomplishing more, working her way towards independence. With the help of her therapists, she continued to set bigger and bigger goals and worked hard towards those milestones. Despite this amazing physical advancement, Sierra was not making such giant strides emotionally yet.

Even though she was experiencing some success with the acupuncture treatments, she still experienced fleeting moments of intense anxiety, and she was still very reliant on us as her family. She did not like to be without one of us close by, and it was important for her to feel safe with people she trusted when she was out of the house. This was logical; as she was becoming more self-aware, she did not like to feel vulnerable.

On March 10th, Sierra had another eye appointment in Boston. This time, Aspen came with us, and we decided to stop and visit the doctors and nurses at Spaulding who had been so instrumental in her recovery journey. We passed through security and headed up to the eighth-floor unit.

As we entered the pediatric ward, the nurse at reception asked how she could help, and before I had a chance to reply,

Sierra's physical therapist was walking by and recognized us … well, she recognized Aspen and me. She stopped and started chatting, and soon, a few more nurses and therapists joined in, all asking about Sierra, wanting to know what she was doing and how she was.

They did not even recognize her. Even with the big smirk on her face as she stood next to us, not saying anything. She really enjoyed fooling them.

Finally, I could no longer contain myself and said, "How's Sierra? Why don't you ask her yourselves?"

Pointing to her on my right, there were gasps and laughter as they stared at her, amazed at the transformation. Then, after the surprise wore off, they asked her lots of questions, wanting to know everything that she had done since she walked out of the hospital only five months ago.

Without missing a beat, Sierra was able to recount all the events and situations she had experienced and things she learned since she left Spaulding. Most impressively, she shared the information clearly and chronologically with those around us. It was an emotional moment, as she had spent a lot of time relearning recall and logical sequencing when telling a story or relating a past event. Seeing her confidently relay every detail with excitement was a milestone.

After we spent some time catching up, we headed down to the waterfront, and the moment I had prayed for all those months ago came true.

Aspen, Sierra, and I walked together along the boardwalk that I had spent many hours looking at just last summer. I wished for the day that I could walk it with both my girls, and here we were, walking along the boardwalk and staring out at the ocean. It was a wonderful afternoon for this mother's heart.

As Sierra became more aware of herself, she became quite self-conscious, and the one thing that kept bothering her was her hair. Sierra had always loved her long hair and was very concerned about her current state, which was still growing back from being half shaved to replace her front piece of skull and remove the staples from the operation. The perfect solution was hair extensions for her.

We inquired at different salons and day spas about the best option for Sierra. To our delight and surprise, a local day spa offered to donate Sierra some hair extensions, and another local salon put them in for free. It was incredible to see how these acts of kindness and generosity from Nadina Pitaro of Epidavros Day Spa and Nicole from Belleza Hair Salon had such an enormous impact on Sierra's self-confidence. She looked and felt great.

And still, she improved. Every week, Sierra accomplished another milestone, and we continued to praise the Almighty Father for his grace and mercy on Sierra and our family.

By mid-March, after much thought and discussion, we put a deposit on an emotional support dog. We knew it would be a while until a puppy would be ready for her, but it was another motivator: her PT was ending at Dartmouth, and it seemed like a natural next step.

That same week, we had a Kripalu Mindful Outdoor Guide named Andrea to offer her time and services to Sierra and our family. Kripalu Mindful Outdoor <u>Learning</u> is grounded in the yogic philosophy that a meaningful connection with nature is as essential part of a balanced and healthy life, another new modality to us. We decided it would be worthwhile to do it.

Sierra (and our whole family) always loved the outdoors, and at this point, I knew that all these generous offers were beneficial to her healing journey, even if we did not fully understand them at the outset. We were willing to try anything that had worked for others in our quest for her continued healing. And if God kept putting these people in front of us, we would keep trying new things.

We met with Andrea on a cold winter's day and went for a guided hike with her, learning about mindful meditation with nature and the way it all relates to us as humans. As we hiked over the icy and uneven terrain, I remember thinking I may have made a mistake as it was extremely slippery on the icy patches and very rocky at times. I was concerned for Sierra and her ability to retain her balance, but she did fantastic! There was not a misstep or slip on her part, which was more than could be said for me.

The weather was gorgeous. It was cold and clear. And being in nature and connecting with the great outdoors in a new way was as exhilarating as it was rejuvenating. At the end of the session, we gathered around a small fire Andrea had built, and she boiled water in a small pot, adding a handful of hemlock leaves and making tea for us to drink together.

It was a very uplifting day, with each of us diving deeper into our connection with nature. Sierra really enjoyed it, too, and was visibly relaxed by the time we got home. She took a nap that afternoon and slept a further ten hours that night. The powerful healing ability of nature made an impact on all of us.

Since the crash, I have learned far more about the brain and TBIs than I ever thought there was knowledge, including how some activities just seem to be hard-wired, activities etched into someone's very fiber that needs no work to retrieve, and in contrast, some other activities are extremely difficult to relearn. Our brains are incredible and amazing, and, as I was learning every day, surprisingly tenacious when guided by the Lord.

One of the most difficult tasks for Sierra was how to tell the time on an analog clock. The numbers and their order threw her off for weeks. Although I wasn't too worried, I put it down to it also being a generational thing - that with all the access to phones and digital devices, she previously had no reason to master an old-fashioned clock face. But then, some activities just flowed for her, like she had never experienced the TBI.

One afternoon, when we were at the Aquatic Center, Aspen convinced Sierra to get in the pool. I was apprehensive as she had not been near the water since the crash, and swimming had not featured anywhere in her therapy sessions. The girls convinced me she would be okay, as all three of us were there, and they would stay in the shallow end.

Sierra really wanted to get in the water, so I told her I would be right at the pool's edge if she changed her mind. In she went. To our surprise (even Sierra's), as soon she got into the pool, it was like instinct took over, and she started swimming like she always had.

There was no noticeable change in her abilities from before the crash; she was elated. As we were discovering, healing from a traumatic brain injury certainly was a continually shifting dynamic of not knowing which knowledge was retained and which needed to be remastered.

Easter was in the first week of April that year, and we celebrated with our extended family with a new perspective on the miracle of resurrection. We took Sierra to view the crash site. She had been curious but also a little fearful about making this trip to recount the events that she remembered about the morning of the crash. We all agreed Easter was the time to do it. Although her memories about a lot of her life and herself were compromised by her TBI, Sierra remembered some things very clearly.

With family and especially Aspen's help, we walked around the tree. Sierra spent a long time looking at the big tree and feeling the huge bald patch on the trunk where her car had torn the bark off the tree. She prayed by the tree for a while, amazed at how strong it was.

Even with the large piece of bark and inner bark torn off, revealing the young sapwood beneath it and the huge ugly gouge of a scar on the trunk from the crash, it still stood majestically in the woods. She felt connected to the strength of the mighty oak. It was a sobering moment for us, the bitter sting of where Sierra's new journey began, and life forever changed for our family in an instant.

It had been important to Sierra and Aspen that she get to participate in as much fun as their senior year had to offer. Sierra had talked a lot about two things since New Year's Day: playing softball with her team again and going to prom.

This was a tremendous motivator for her, so Steven and I made the decision early on to let Sierra decide what she would like to do. It had been suggested again that having her participate in so many social events could delay her progress. They suggested it would be better for her to only focus on her therapies.

However, as her family and the people who knew her best, we knew that if she got something in her head, she would work until it was hers. A lot of Sierra was different, but this was one of those parts of her that remained unchanged. She was always our strong-willed warrior child both before and after the crash.

Parental instinct also knew that the richness of being able to be a teen and being social and participating in all the things she loved, to be a high school senior doing all the fun stuff she saw Aspen doing, was a driving force for her. She and Aspen had always done everything together. There was no way she was missing out on this. She was determined to experience it all, and we were determined to help her get there.

The week after Easter, Sierra, Aspen, and I went dress shopping for the prom with some friends. The girls laughed, joked, and giggled excitedly as they tried on dresses and picked out dresses for each other. It was so wonderful to hear Aspen and Sierra chattering and laughing with each other like they used to when they were much younger.

They both settled on long gowns with flowing floor-length skirts and fitted bodices. Sierra's dress was navy blue with silver detailing and was a halter style. Aspen's dress was ivory and white with spaghetti straps. The girls both looked so beautiful, and I was as excited as they were, grateful because even four months ago, it did not seem possible that Sierra would be able to go to the prom and dance and have fun with a date. We were ecstatic.

As winter's long grip on Vermont gave way to spring, the girls and I took a trip to Home Depot to buy some mulch for our garden. Watching Sierra lift and load the bulky bags of mulch with Aspen made me so proud of how far she had come.

I am certain I was the only one shedding a tear and offering a prayer of gratitude in the parking lot that morning. Thinking about how hard she had worked to get to do a regular Saturday morning activity was humbling. I was incredibly grateful and overcome by God's endless blessings on Sierra and our family.

Sierra also really wanted to go back and play softball; it was something she missed a lot since the crash. Aspen supported this 110%; they had always been on the same team, and neither of them could imagine it being any different this year. One day in March, I couldn't find either of the girls in the house and thought they were in one of their bedrooms looking at their phones.

I was astonished when I looked out the window to see Sierra and Aspen playing catch in the yard! This was a triumph all by itself. Both girls were sure this was a sign that Sierra was going to be able to play. We agreed to call the coaches and let her try out. A week after moving mulch at Home Depot, the varsity softball season started, and even though it did not seem like a reality for her in January, Sierra was mentally ready to play by mid-April.

After contacting her coaches, Chuck and Josh, they invited her to the makeshift batting cage that was set up at her high school gym to see if it was something she could realistically do.

As we watched in the gym, we were excited and nervous for her. She had worked so hard to gain control of her body, but could she do this? Would her instinct and muscle memory shine through? Sierra was feeling a lot of anxiety as she stepped into the cage.

Josh started off throwing her soft pitches for her to get a feel for it again, and she hit the ball immediately, which visibly eased her apprehension. The effect on us was electric. We could not help ourselves, yelling and cheering for her. With each pitch, we could see her returning to her old self, worried less about her form and more about hitting the ball.

She wasn't just tapping it, either. These were powerful line drives she was smashing to the back of the cage. As she stepped out of the cage, elated, Chuck and Josh said they were convinced, and she announced she wanted to play.

A few days later, Sierra and Steven joined the team for practice. Per Vermont Principals Association rules, Sierra had to complete ten practices before she could play in a game. Steven worked with Sierra alongside the girls' practices until she was strong and capable enough to participate in the drills with the rest of the team. Extraordinary effort was also made by both Chuck and Josh to work with her individually to have her (and us) feeling confident and comfortable with her softball skills before she took the field.

Exactly ten months to the day of Sierra's crash, she went up to bat. The pitcher threw the ball over the plate, and Sierra swung and hit the ball! She ran to first base, just beating the throw from the right fielder. She then got to second and third bases on singles, and then on the next hit, she crossed home plate! When she crossed home plate, Aspen met her in the on-deck circle for a big hug.

The entire field was cheering. Almost every member of our family and some fans were in tears, elated, yelling and cheering for her. It was an incredible play! Just 14 days prior to this ecstatic event, Sierra graduated from her outpatient PT at Dartmouth.

Sierra felt great doing something she enjoyed again. The varsity softball team went on to win the Division III championship, with Aspen catching the game-winning ball. It was a memorable season for both of my girls!

By this time, the "Miracle for Sierra – God's Heros Unite" Facebook page had over 3,500 members. It was mind-boggling that the page continued to grow. So many people with so many prayers and good intentions lifting us daily often gave us the energy to keep going on particularly long and tiring days. They were simply heaven-sent.

The month of May brought National EMS Week, which is the week to honor our frontline heroes dedicated to providing emergency medicine that saves so many lives every day. Sierra had been planning for us to honor the twenty-three first responders for a few months now. I was impressed that her memory was getting stronger, and she was growing more confident in her communication.

She was less confused and forgetful. By now, Sierra had been receiving acupuncture treatments for several weeks, and I started to notice that she was becoming remarkably more independent, which was very encouraging. When she did have an anxiety attack, it was shorter, and she could self-regulate a lot faster.

Sierra was excited to be able to thank the volunteer fire department, as well as the first responders and emergency services personnel who worked so hard to save her life and get her to the hospital. She couldn't wait to show them how well she was doing.

Lance and Melissa Battersby from The Newbury Village Store graciously offered to host the event, and we invited all the people who were there at the scene of the crash that day, from EMS to firefighters, state troopers, and the DART helicopter team, as well as the witnesses and first people on the scene.

May 19th, 2021, was a sunny late spring day, and Burlington, Vermont's WCAX had sent a reporter and cameraperson to cover the event. We celebrated by showing them a video of Sierra's recovery, giving them Sierra Strong t-shirts and bracelets as well, and buying them all lunch of pizza and cake.

It was a meaningful and touching event. Even though it was very draining for her, Sierra made her best effort to speak with all twenty-three people. It was important to her that she got to thank them all for being there that day.

Steven and I also talked to many of the first responders, and in the process, we learned so many more incredible details about the scene and the day of the crash. They were all amazed at the miracle of Sierra's recovery; after seeing the devastation and debris at the crash site, and Sierra herself with zero-oxygen saturation in the helicopter, and that the golden hour, which is the most critical for successful emergency treatment, had passed by the time she got to the hospital.

They all agreed that the fact that she survived and then thrived was simply a miracle. The main thing that stands out from those conversations is the fact that nobody expected her to live. Many of them admitted that they (the EMS staff) had been expecting a text before the end of the day of the crash letting them know she had passed. Between them, they had around 150 years of experience, and none of them had ever seen a survivor from a scene like that.

They spoke to us at length about how miraculous it was, almost not believing they were looking at the same girl. One of them even mentioned that God himself must have been looking out for her that day. Again, I had a small insight into how regularly traumatic EMS workers' jobs were, especially the car crashes, and I could appreciate their grateful attitude for both Sierra's recovery and the gesture from our family.

Steven's dad had been a volunteer in the fire department for thirty years, and his brother had been with them for ten years, so we knew very well how personal such a role was in a small-town community, where almost everyone knows the victim, or the family, connected to a horrible crash. It felt good to be able to share a survival story with them.

The last week of May, we started planning for the twins' graduation party, which would be held on their grandparents' land, where Sierra's healing garden was located. We started prepping for the occasion. Their graduation day was only a month away!

Due to COVID restrictions, the senior high school class did not have their Fall Festival in November, so it was replaced with a Spring Fling at the end of May. It was held at the school with a dance, food, seasonal festivities, and a bonfire. Sierra and Aspen both went and had the best time! They were ecstatic that they could do these things together like they had planned for years before the crash.

Our home was filled with positive energy and love. This was enhanced by Lindsay, our eldest daughter, and her fiancé announcing that they were expecting a baby in January 2022. We were all so excited! God was showering us with multiple blessings.

At the beginning of June, someone recommended another therapy to try for Sierra: Hyperbaric Oxygen Therapy (HBOT). This therapy involves breathing pure oxygen in a pressurized environment and has been used for years in treating decompression illness. It often affects divers.

It has recently been utilized in treating brain injuries as it helps the brain create new capillaries around the damaged ones, increasing blood flow to those areas of the brain. It has also been proven to assist in the treatment of PTSD, carbon monoxide poisoning, radiation necrosis, gangrene, and other wound healing.

Although it's still in the early days of studying the exact effectiveness of HBOT on TBI patients, there was enough anecdotal evidence that made Steven and I think it was worth a try. I traveled five days a week for her to participate in the therapy. She would lay in a hyperbaric chamber and breathe pure oxygen for an hour at a time.

By this time, we had tried multiple therapies on Sierra, and most of them had a positive effect to some extent, but the ones that were a success made a noticeable difference in her recovery. This therapy was incredibly beneficial for Sierra, although the acupuncture had helped too with the combination of the HBOT completely removed her brain fog and stabilized her emotions, giving her more clarity to process information. It was an outstanding success in her treatment journey.

Sierra was also referred to a Transformational Specialist by her primary care provider, which brought us into contact with Gretchen Moulton. As a trained former physical therapist and nutritionist, she would offer a very specific look at transforming Sierra's diet and how it may be affecting her health.

We chatted over the phone and set a time for her to come to the house for an initial consultation the following week. I was not sure if Sierra was quite at the place to be able to fully utilize nutrition advice, but I knew she was close.

As it turned out, Gretchen came over the week of prom, and the energy in our home was buzzing. She told me later that she had been nervous to meet us, but the high energy of the girls in the throes of excitement for their Senior end-of-year activities and softball was very distracting.

I could see she was a very sincere and genuine person who took her role quite seriously and that she seemed to connect with Sierra in a very natural way. As we easily chatted, Gretchen asked us how we felt about the metaphysical and if she could ask Sierra some questions about being in a coma.

We shared that we believed in the metaphysical and agreed, so Gretchen cautiously asked about Sierra's meeting with God.

Sierra lit up with excitement, "Yes! Yes!" and then a confused, "How did you know?"

Especially since we had not discussed who and what she saw in a coma with anyone outside of our immediate family, Gretchen said she had witnessed it in a vision and was willing to help Sierra with her nutrition and as far as she wanted to go on that journey. We decided to move forward with Transformational Coaching and made Sierra's first official appointment for later in July.

Chapter Thirteen – Blessings

> 7 The LORD *is* my strength and my shield;
> My heart trusted in Him, and I am helped;
> Therefore my heart greatly rejoices,
> And with my song I will praise Him. Psalms 28:7

June 17th, 2021, was the day of the prom, and the excitement in our home was palpable. Sierra and Aspen spent the afternoon having their nails, hair, and make-up done. Both girls looked amazing and so beautiful in their dresses. Their dates also looked handsome in their suits. Aspen went with her boyfriend, and Sierra's date was a longtime friend. They all looked so grown up.

It was hard to believe that they were already heading off to senior prom. Their school years up until that point seemed to have passed by us in the blink of an eye. We took photos before they left, and by far, my favorite photos are of the four of them goofing around on the lawn outside our home. Seeing Sierra's excitement and confidence was heartwarming and a very definite sign that her brain was healing beyond every expected outcome.

Prom night was a huge success. Sierra and Aspen danced and talked and hung out with their dates and friends all night, returning home close to midnight, exhausted and satisfied. They then stayed up into the small hours, talking and recounting events of the night. It was the latest Sierra had been up in nearly a year, and she relished every minute.

A couple of weeks after prom, it was their Class of 2021 Graduation. Keeping with tradition, the senior class chose one teacher to represent them in a speech. This year, it was Sierra and Aspen's physics teacher, Mrs. Carson, who is one of Oxbow's favorite science teachers. Everybody loves Mrs. Carson; she is a kindhearted and intelligent individual loved by all her students.

Her speech to the senior class was incredibly inspiring and true to her pragmatic nature, not clichéd or cheesy, which is something the students love about her. Before she closed, she recognized the strength of our family and provided her accurate and touching observations of Aspen and Sierra's support for one another. This was a beautifully accurate observation and will never be forgotten.

Next was the presentation of diplomas, and when it was Sierra's turn to walk unassisted on stage to collect her diploma, the audience erupted with cheers and whistles and a standing ovation. The principal gave her a huge hug, and there was not a dry eye in our family. Steven and I were so proud of our girls. Their high school graduation will be etched in our memories forever.

The following weekend was the graduation party, held on their grandparents' land, with their friends and friends' families and our extended family all attending. So many people came and shared the joy and celebrated with us. The weather was perfect, and the whole weekend was joyous and festive.

It was wonderful to celebrate the girl's graduation together. Considering that the school year had started, we did not imagine that Sierra would be walking and talking, let alone graduating high school together with Aspen. We were humbled and in awe of the grace of God, granting Sierra miracle after miracle to get to this point.

The week after graduation, we finally got to take our family vacation to Old Orchard Beach, Maine, where we had been planning to go on July 8th the previous year before our plans were dramatically changed by Sierra's crash. To say we felt excited was an understatement. At last, our long-awaited family beach vacation had arrived!

The weather was sublime, and we quickly fell into our relaxed beach/vacation schedule, waking up early to walk down to the beach and watch the sunrise, look for sand dollars, and take a few moments to contemplate the coming day.

One morning, as we wandered down the beach in the lifting gloom, we drifted off to the activities we were drawn to, whether it was striding through the sand, walking at the water's edge, or just sitting in the cool sand, drinking hot coffee and watching the sky get lighter. Steven and Sierra went looking for sand dollars, wading out knee-deep in the predawn grey and blue shadows. I walked along the water's edge, watching them in the calm water, bent over at the waist, Sierra never straying too far from her dad.

We joked about how futile it was, that all the sand dollars had gone, as we never found more than a few between us all. It was a good-natured family competition we had carried on for ten years or so, and it was always a good start to the day when you found the most, which was usually only one or two. The symbolism that sand dollars represent has always resonated deeply with me - rebirth, renewal, and transformation.

However, as I started to wander down the beach, I kept hearing Sierra shouting and laughing triumphantly as she found another and then another. By the time we got back together and I asked her how many she had found, it was over sixty sand dollars of all sizes and colors! They were stuffed in her pockets and overflowing from her arms. It was as if they had all been gravitating towards her.

None of us had ever seen or found so many together as a family at one time, never mind alone! It made sense that Sierra would naturally attract the very symbol of what she had lived through over the last year.

Our 2021 family vacation was memorable for so many reasons, and we finally got to wear the "Life is Better Around the Campfire - Longmoore Adventure 2020" t-shirts I had made in anticipation of our vacation the year before. And we got to take our traditional family photos, regular and goofy, with all fourteen of us wearing our shirts.

Returning home, we felt rested and rejuvenated, layers of stress loosened from the previous twelve months. I have realized when you experience such events as we had with Sierra and the crash, besides the obvious changes a family experiences, there is an added unspoken layer of trepidation psychologically, and even when you think it's all OK and you are all doing well, it's not until you get a chance to just enjoy your time with each other that you see how much tension had remained.

In her last few months at school, Sierra had been working with a vocational rehabilitation team in preparation for when she graduated. They continued working with her after the school year was done and helped her with her first job search.

They were a fantastic boost to Sierra's self-esteem, and she quickly found a job, working at Kendal in Hanover, which is a retirement community on the Connecticut River, in Dining Services. They were welcoming and supportive of Sierra, knowing of her TBI healing journey, and they were very encouraging. She started working part-time, doing short shifts while she was becoming more confident.

As her stamina and confidence increased, they worked with her to extend her working day in small increments until she was working full shifts. It was a huge boost to her confidence, and she quickly made friends with some of her workmates.

With the first anniversary of her crash fast approaching, Sierra wanted to raise money for a Massachusetts-based nonprofit organization called "Unify Against Bullying." This foundation is very near to her heart. Having experienced the continual intimidation from her ex, she knew firsthand how hard it is to speak up.

Their message of ending the silence resonated with our entire family, so we all decided to participate with her. We sold t-shirts and bracelets and matched whatever money was raised. We sold them online through "The Miracle for Sierra – God's Hero's Unite" Facebook page and in person, raising $1,000 in just a few weeks.

With our matching contribution, we donated $2,000 to this cause. Sierra and I were featured in an interview for their annual fundraiser to inspire others to donate, too. Sierra found the whole experience very satisfying, and we spoke of her desire to be able to start something like that to help people in similar ways. This was the new big-hearted Sierra, always aware of the help others needed on so many levels and wanting to show love to them all. We started seriously talking about ways she could do this.

Wanting some way to mark the anniversary of the crash day personally, we decided the best way to do this was to go to the tree in the morning to say prayers and reflect on the past year. We met early at the tree and circled it, making a human chain, twelve of us holding hands as we each gave solemn testimony about what we had experienced and learned in the 365 days since the crash occurred.

We prayed and cried and talked about our fears and what we were grateful for and hugged and gave thanks to God for walking with Sierra through all of it. It was a somber morning of remembrance for us. We continued with the various recommended therapies to continue Sierra's healing journey, and Sierra's first appointment with Gretchen, the transformational coach, was not too long after the first anniversary of the crash.

As Gretchen liked to keep the first appointment informal to assist in building a relationship with her client, on that day, she had to take her car to the dealership about an hour away. She suggested she pick up Sierra and take her to lunch. It would be a great way for them to get to know each other and for Gretchen to gauge where Sierra was at with her food and nutritional preferences.

It was the first time Sierra would be in a car with someone other than family and out of sight since the crash. We talked to Sierra about it, and she thought it would be OK. She liked Gretchen, and we trusted her.

We also reminded ourselves that if God had trusted her enough to show her a vision of Sierra's meeting with Him, surely, we could trust her too. Besides, Sierra was going to have to start being able to go places on her own again, and this was a good start.

It still did not diminish the feelings of fear and concern watching them drive away. Steven was especially nervous about letting her go. The whole family had become very protective of her, especially her dad. Gretchen saw the look of fear and dread on his face as they pulled out of the driveway but had not realized until later the significance of that first official appointment with Sierra.

They had a productive first meeting, and Gretchen delivered Sierra safely home, with another appointment scheduled for the following week. It was a good experience for all concerned, and it let Sierra know she could leave the house safely without us, which was invaluable.

Later in July, Lindsay, Aspen, Sierra, and I went dress shopping for Lindsay's upcoming wedding. We were all so excited to get to hang out together, as it didn't happen very often since Lindsay had left home, gotten engaged, and worked full-time.

She was busy with her own life these days. We had lunch and shopped and spent the afternoon excitedly shopping and discussing the wedding. To know Sierra would be able to stand up proudly and with confidence at her sister's wedding was a much-anticipated moment for all of us.

It was phenomenal seeing Sierra accomplish all these milestones. She went from strength to strength almost daily. We stopped anticipating anything less than a full recovery some months ago, and she was on track to achieve exactly that. A full recovery.

We continued to pray and give thanks, so grateful to God for all his blessings. To see Sierra come so much farther than was ever medically thought possible and witnessing the continual flow of miracles, Steven and I knew our family had been incredibly and abundantly blessed.

Emotionally, though, sometimes things can be tough. As a mother, the instinct is to ease the burden you see your children carry, but that is not often possible. While I was proud of our town and community and so very grateful for the support Sierra and our family had been shown from all sections of the community, it could be heartbreaking and frustrating at times, too, seeing the way Sierra was treated as she worked hard to get integrated back into "regular life."

Seeing some people who had known her before the crash treat her so differently made me feel emotional and angry at times. While I could understand because she did look different and moved and spoke differently, she was still Sierra! She had worked so hard to be independent and was more than capable; she had literally come back from death's door.

Yet the way some people who had previously been close to our family started avoiding us or treating her like a baby was tough to deal with. It was also difficult to see people's true characters revealed in the aftermath of the crash. Although I must admit, I found it much harder to deal with than Sierra did. I had expected so much more from some people who turned their backs on us.

It was incredibly disappointing. Yet God has a way of balancing the scales, and there were people we hardly knew before the crash whose grace, kindness, and generosity of spirit have firmly connected them to our family since July 2020. The outpouring of authenticity from previous strangers has truly added a depth to our friendships that we had not experienced before.

Sierra continued to receive inspiration and well wishes from amazing people who had also experienced incredible healing journeys. A week after the game, Sierra received a special video message from Melissa Stockwell, a Paralympian who was competing in the Tokyo Olympics that year. Melissa was on active duty in Iraq in 2004 when her vehicle was hit by a roadside bomb, and she became the first female American soldier to lose a limb.

Her message was inspiring and personal. Sierra and I were moved by the sentiment that she was able to see the abilities of her disability. It resonated deeply within me. We watched every event she competed in Tokyo, cheering and celebrating, fully invested in this inspirational athlete, feeling a real connection with her.

Shortly after receiving the video message from Melissa and seeing her compete in the Paralympics, Sierra was inspired to start creating her own videos to share with the Facebook group to keep everyone updated on how she was doing, what she had been up to, and to thank everyone for their ongoing prayers and support. She really enjoyed this process, and it was encouraging to watch her confidence in communication grow with each video.

As I mentioned earlier, one of the things I was so grateful for that remained unchanged in Sierra was her creativity. This was a massive relief, as we had been told over and over with all the damage she sustained to her brain, there was a chance she would not still have the same creative impulses. And then they said the same thing when she struggled to hold a pencil and even connect it to a piece of paper.

We heard it again as she gained more control and could draw simple, scratchy figures and scenes. Steven and I were initially concerned she may lose the desire to create art the way she once had, as she was starting over, but much to our delight, her inherent artistic ability was still present, even more pronounced than before. This became more obvious as the months went by, and she continued to draw and create and get better and more competent with each project she undertook. That summer, she worked hard on a full-sized ceramic lion head she designed for Steven's birthday.

It was remarkable, and the detail she captured in the colors of the lion's mane and face was majestic. It was so beautiful when she was done. She was so proud of it. It symbolized her father, the Protector. He has always told her, "Do not worry about who is in front of you. Because I will always be behind you." This has always given her great comfort and security.

In August, we surprised the kids with a trip to Boston for a Red Sox game. Sierra had always loved all sports, and until the crash, she had been a year-round athlete, playing soccer in the fall, basketball in the winter, and softball in the spring since she was in elementary school. It was great to be able to go to a game.

It was an exciting game, too, and for the first time in her recovery, strangers treated her completely normally. As her mother and the person who has been alongside her through all stages of her healing journey, I could see that going to the game and just feeling like a normal family out together in public was a much-needed break and gave me some hope that Sierra would achieve that full recovery and there would be a point in the near future that people would never be able to tell she had experienced a severe TBI.

August also saw Aspen and Sierra start online university courses. Both with the view to attending full-time at some point in the future. Sierra started her course through the local community college, which she enjoyed and was happy to be doing. After some contemplation, the end of August also saw her begin a driver's rehabilitation program in Burlington, Vermont.

At first, Sierra had felt anxious about driving, wanting one of us to be with her all the time in a vehicle, but we could tell she was healing when she started talking about being able to drive herself once more.

Even if she didn't want to do it right away, it was encouraging that she did see herself doing it sometime in the future. Ever aware that after such a devastating crash, she could be paralyzed with fear at the thought of driving by herself again, we were happy to let her take the lead. This was a big step for her.

We also heard that the puppy we put a deposit on back in March had been born! A Siberian husky, he was one of fourteen puppies from two litters. It was still two months before we would be able to pick him up, but Sierra was super excited he had been born. It was only a matter of time until he was hers!

Realizing our newfound love for attending live games, we decided to include football and surprised the kids again in September with tickets to the New England Patriots 2021 season-opening game at Gillette Stadium in Foxboro, Massachusetts. We decided to head down early and attend mass at St Mary's Church, which is a famous catholic church not too far from Gillette Stadium.

I felt compelled to attend like our family was drawn there. The church is over 150 years old and so majestic. At the back of the church, there is a huge live tree growing in the church, almost reaching the ceiling, and in the middle of the tree is a statue of Blessed Mother Mary, which is exquisitely beautiful. I was enthralled. I had heard about it, but seeing it in front of me was incredible.

I walked to the back to take a better look. Just in front of the tree was a small table, where there would usually be prayer cards and small informational pamphlets, etc., for visitors to take with them and use in their worship.

On that morning, the table only held one single prayer card, and I was drawn to it immediately. It was a depiction of Jesus with vibrant ice-blue eyes. Ever since Sierra had told us about His remarkable vibrant blue eyes, I had tried to imagine the intensity, and here He was, looking straight at me with those eyes! I still have the prayer card and keep it tucked in the visor in my car.

We left the church feeling uplifted and filled with excitement for the rest of the day. We continued to the game, which was incredible. It was a nail-biting, electrifying game that the Patriots lost by one point. The stadium was buzzing. We all had so much fun; it was another great day as a family, where nobody even looked twice at us. We were coming to appreciate this new normal.

Trying to surprise a teenager when they are expecting something is no mean feat, and a couple of weeks later, after being in contact with the breeder of the puppy, we had secretly arranged a pickup. We had been evading Sierra's questions for a month or so, with vague answers whenever she would ask about the arrival of the puppy.

As the breeder had moved from Vermont to Kentucky, we kept telling her there were travel details to sort out and that we were thinking about driving to Kentucky for a weekend to get the pup. This idea had originally been on the cards, but instead, the breeder had decided to head up to the area with the puppies, as many of the buyers were still around our area.

Steven and I had to go over to West Lebanon, in New Hampshire, to run some errands and get a few things done. It was a quiet day at home, and we suggested Sierra came with us for the ride. After running the errands, Steven "remembered" just one more stop, and we pulled into the parking lot of Best Buy.

The breeder had driven the fourteen Siberian Husky puppies up in a van and had the side door open. There was a small crowd of people, and as we pulled in, Sierra wanted to know what was happening, so we decided to go over to look. As we got closer, there was lots of excited chatter mixed with puppy yips and barks. Sierra gasped, staring at us with her mouth open and then bursting with joy as she comprehended the scene in front of her.

"Am I getting my puppy today??!" She was elated.

Finally, her own puppy was here. Steven and I had genuinely surprised her. We planned to raise him with us in the family until he was a year old, and then he would start training to be a service dog for Sierra. She cuddled his crate the whole way home.

Lindsay's wedding was in the first week of October. Sierra and Tristan walked and stood together during the ceremony, and even though it was a grey, foggy fall afternoon, everything went off without a hitch, and the ceremony was heartfelt and beautiful. Tristan's friend Hayden also came, and he and Sierra danced and hung out, as was becoming the nature of their friendship at these things.

I had a moment of pure love and elation that this was even happening, reflecting on the fact that a mere year ago, Sierra had been preparing to leave Spaulding and had already come so far, but we had not realized the extent of the miracles still before her.

Steven and I were incredibly proud parents, with all our children have grown and experienced so much in the last year. Here they all were so beautiful and grown up, the wedding was a wonderful celebration. It was a great weekend to start a new chapter and an addition to our family.

Chapter Fourteen – Joyful Seasons

[45] Blessed *is* she who believed, for there will be a fulfillment of those things which were told her from the Lord." **Luke 1:45**

Before we knew it, the holidays were upon us again, and my brother Vincent joined us from Buffalo as usual for Thanksgiving. It was a busy yet fulfilling few days, again full of gratitude, food, and enjoying the time with family. The weekend after Thanksgiving, we kept with our family tradition and drove to the tree farm in New Hampshire for our annual tree selection and harvesting.

The difference in Sierra's strength and cognitive abilities was striking. She was keeping up with Aspen as if it was the most normal thing in the world because it was. My brother was impressed and mentioned how much more confident and independent Sierra was. He had not seen her for a little over six months and was so proud of the changes he saw in his niece.

True to the lasting effects of experiencing a brain injury, she still had moments of intense anxiety but could recognize her body's response without shutting down. Due to the therapies she had learned from, she moved through them quicker and recovered faster than the year before. It was a lovely holiday, full of love for family and our lives, and we continued to be grateful for everything God had blessed us with.

The excitement of Lindsay's wedding preparations had eaten up the Fall months quickly, so we decided to take our annual trip to the Padre Pio Center in Pennsylvania the first weekend of December. It was still doubtful if we would make it, however, as Lindsay had experienced all sorts of pregnancy complications and had been in and out of hospital often, including the week before we were due to go.

As her mom, I wanted to be available for my first baby girl and her first baby if she needed me. Lindsay was sure everything would be fine as she was scheduled to go home the day we were heading to Pennsylvania. She knew how important the pilgrimage to the Padre Pio Center was to us and insisted we go.

The center was a six-hour drive from our home in Vermont, and we headed out early on Friday morning, aiming to get there by mid-morning so we could spend most of the day at the Center. When we were only about an hour away from Barto, the town where the Padre Pio Center is located, Lindsay called to let us know they had decided to induce her that afternoon, and the baby would be born two months prematurely. This was an emotional blow for us hundreds of miles and hours away.

We pulled over to the side of the road, and Steven led us in prayer, asking God what we should do. Even though Aspen and I were upset and worried, Sierra was extremely calm. She felt certain that God had Lindsay and the baby safely in his care.

We realized Lindsay was well cared for, and her husband was with her, and that we would not be able to be present anyway due to the COVID regulations still enforced in the neo-natal and delivery wards. After weighing up the situation and discussing all options, we decided the best thing to do would be to continue to the Padre Pio Center and drive back the next day instead of Sunday as originally planned.

This moment stands out in my mind as it represents how far we had come and how different we were as a family. Before the crash, we would have all panicked, wanting to get back to being within a reasonable distance as soon as possible. But after everything we had experienced since July 2020, even though we were concerned, our reactions were now of genuine faith, knowing that God is in control, and after some quiet time in prayer, we were happy to listen and let Him lead.

Our visit to the Padre Pio Center was extra special that year. After the benediction mass, they brought out one of Padre Pio's relic gloves that he wore for fifty years over his hands to cover the open wounds, as he had been marked by the stigmata from 1918 until his death in 1968.

They invited people to come up and pray over the glove, which we did, praying fervently for Lindsay and the baby's safe delivery. We ended that visit feeling humbled and honored to receive the privilege of being in the presence of the spirit of St. Padre Pio and one of his relics. We were certainly blessed that day. As a practicing Catholic, it is not often you get the opportunity to see a relic, let alone pray over one.

Baby Ava Reese was born early Friday evening, December 3rd, at only 2.8 pounds. Mother and baby were healthy and doing well. Ava had strong vitals but was at risk as she was so premature. She was small but fierce, just like her Aunt Sierra. Ava would remain in the NICU for two months until she could go home.

It was around this time that a friend from the Midwest sent me an article about the incredible results people were experiencing with stem cell therapy. Stem cell therapy seemed so radical and was not approved by the FDA, even though it had been used successfully for many years. Steven and I did not know what to think, but we were curious, and so we did some research of our own.

What we learned was intriguing, discovering that as an invasive form of regenerative medicine, it repairs damaged cells by isolating and using the body's own cells, reducing inflammation and modulating the immune system. It could be used to treat a variety of medical conditions, such as autoimmune, inflammatory, and neurological disorders.

It seemed like Sierra would be a perfect candidate for this treatment. Reminding ourselves that we had been divinely guided concerning various therapies for Sierra up until this point, we prayed about it, evaluated our research, and decided it would be worth doing for her.

There are only two clinics in the United States that perform this therapy. Both are out west, one in Colorado and one in Arizona. After initial inquiries, we decided to go to Arizona and scheduled her treatment for March 2022. The procedure consisted of extracting Sierra's own cells and spinning them to isolate the white blood cells.

The body's white blood cells vibrate very quickly, and as we age, the cells slow down to the point where movement is barely perceptible. Sierra's white blood cells still vibrated at a very high rate, which was an excellent sign that the therapy had a high chance of success.

Her own stem cells were then injected into her nasal cavity and lower back. The procedure takes a patient's own cells and injects them into the bone marrow to facilitate healthy cell production, which the body then uses to repair the damaged areas.

With a rigorous follow-up routine involving nasal spray to assist with the breakdown of the atrophy experienced in the frontal lobe and a super vitamin supplement which also contained growth hormone to support her immune system and encourage healthy cell production, we left the clinic knowing there would be some significant changes to her overall healing but did not realize the depth and extent of this process.

As soon as we returned from Arizona, we reenrolled Sierra in hyperbaric oxygen therapy again to assist in purifying and strengthening the new cells that her body was producing.

About four weeks after the treatment, we started to see some big changes in Sierra.

As her brain adjusted to the influx of healthy cells, it started establishing the neural pathways that her brain had circumvented because of the crash. Yes, her brain had healed, but it had developed new pathways of memory and learning, completely avoiding the damaged areas.

The stem cells started to break down the scar tissue and reconnect the neural pathways correctly, which meant (in a nutshell) the healing and cognitive work that had been completed was now being directed differently.

This became a regressive experience for all of us, with the issues and challenges we thought we had already faced and overcome resurfacing with a vengeance. Sierra experienced frustration, sadness, and grief all over again. She had to relearn how to self-regulate and deal with the memories that would sweep over her like a thunderstorm or flood.

It was difficult for both her and us. Unexpected triggers would cause her to suffer intense anxiety from sheer frustration or remembering what she used to be able to do, as opposed to how she viewed herself now.

During this time, Sierra was still attending speech therapy at Dartmouth Hitchcock Medical Center, and her speech therapist, noticing the difficulties Sierra was re-experiencing, suggested we investigate a neurofeedback program for her. Neurofeedback is a potentially powerful set of techniques that trains the brain to use its own resources to self-regulate.

It is non-invasive and comfortable as the brain learns to modify its own functioning by receiving feedback about its current state and being rewarded for changing its state. Published studies attest to its effectiveness for many disorders and psychological problems.

In the neurofeedback training, the patient sits comfortably and plays a video game that is controlled entirely by their brain. The computer sets goals, and the game responds to the control from the brain, pausing when time is needed to figure it out or progressing as they control it with ease.

Through visual and audio feedback, the brain is rewarded with the goal of developing new pathways and being able to activate those patterns when it needs to. They can be set to exercise the brain to develop patterns that improve attention, mood, or sleep or that decrease impulsivity, anger, pain, or other psychological symptoms. They scan the brain regularly to see where exactly it is re-pathing and what was firing and when.

She started the treatment in the New Year, and at the beginning, Sierra's brain scan showed us something fascinating about her brain waves. Her alpha and beta waves had reversed; usually, the alpha waves are measured predominantly at the front of the brain and the beta waves at the back of the brain. The vibrations of each had switched, with the alpha vibration now reading in the beta area and the beta waves now reading in the front or alpha area of the brain.

The doctor was surprised, as the activity of both waves was a lot more than usually expected from a TBI patient. However, as we have learned, the brain is a miraculous part of our body, often healing itself in ways that defy science or medical reasoning. The doctor mentioned because of this switch in her brain wave activity.

It was as if her crown chakra, which is one of the seven energy centers in the body that corresponds to physio-emotional functions, was empowered to allow spiritual connections to flow freely. This made complete sense to us, as since Sierra had returned home from Spaulding, there had been multiple times she had seen and heard things around the house that we did not.

She often told us of shadow people or spirits she had seen. Sierra was never afraid of them; they were just something she could see and we could not. She worked with a spiritual life coach to learn how to ask if they were of God or of evil. Although as she healed over time and her connection to her physical world strengthened, she lost some of this spiritual sight.

Driving again had been something on Sierra's (and our) minds for a while, and we had been taking her over to Burlington to attend driver rehabilitation classes for months. This was a big deal for her and us, too. We completely understood if she never wanted to get behind the wheel of a car again.

Although she was hesitant at first, her resiliency and determination grew as she attended the classes and completed extensive visual PT. Sierra again proved her warrior spirit could overcome anything. She re-sat her license and started driving again. It was an exciting day in our house, and it was wonderful to see her feeling so proud of herself.

It was bittersweet for Steven and me, though, but like everything else she had done so far, we were proud of how hard she had worked to be able to drive again. Seeing her overcome her fear of driving was a huge boost to her confidence and desire to be "just normal" again. In retrospect, however, it was not too different from the worry we feel for any of our kids driving. More so now that we have experienced how quickly a car crash can change the course of an entire family.

July 2022 marked the two-year anniversary of the crash, and we celebrated Sierra's journey as we had the first year by gathering at the tree on Snake Rd. Sierra wanted the theme to be: God is greater than our ups and downs. She also wanted the community to spread acts of kindness to others.

We had signs made and left them around the community for people to pick up and take with them to include in a picture of them doing simple acts of kindness and post to Sierra's Miracle Facebook page. We were heartened at how many people did this, with many posts of kindness making it on the page.

The "Miracle for Sierra - God's Heroes Unite" Facebook page had developed into a beautifully supportive community, with hundreds of prayer warriors and many other requests from devastated families whose loved ones had been injured or were very sick.

The way everyone pulls together – most being complete strangers, lifting each other selflessly in prayer and with love and respect is wonderful. It provides so much comfort and support for so many and is truly a gift from above. I feel privileged to have been led to start something so positive.

Through the course of her therapies and since leaving Spaulding, Sierra had made friends with other TBI survivors. Often sending them artwork and encouragement. This bonded her with several young adults who, like her, had their lives irrevocably altered by a TBI.

She would support them however she could, knowing first-hand how tough it is to reclaim independence and a sense of self after experiencing such an injury. In the summer of 2022, she supported one of her friends, participating in a fund-raiser for him. This solidifies her desire to be able to offer tools and support for vulnerable, invisible sections of our communities.

Life gradually balanced out for us as we all adjusted to the changes and situations that the course of life brings. We took our annual Maine summer vacation, which was a wonderful break, as it always has been. Our extended family getting to unwind and decompress together is a tradition we all look forward to. We also got the joyful news that Tristan's fiancé Danielle was pregnant! Sierra was so excited! She loved spending time with her niece Ava and couldn't wait to meet another niece or nephew!

August came and brought the biggest adjustment of all for the twins. It was moving day and time for Aspen to move away to attend college. It was the first time in nineteen years that the girls had lived apart from each other. Aspen had worked hard to get into a Division I college and, as a student-athlete, deserved the opportunity and everything it brought for her.

It was still a very difficult transition for the girls. Sierra was sad and took a while to adjust, but she carried on with her own online studies at the community college and worked towards being able to attend in-person part-time. She also focused on actively talking about her journey and raising awareness about TBI with her supporters every chance she had. Her courage and self-confidence were extremely high when she was talking to people about her journey and educating and supporting people. It was, and still is, very important to her.

In September, Sierra and I decided to attend a Love Your Brain retreat in Maine. The Love Your Brain organization was started by Vermont's own Olympic snowboarder, Kevin Pearce after he recovered from a traumatic brain injury sustained in training before the 2010 Vancouver Winter Olympics.

As he recovered, he and his family felt an outpouring of love and support from their own community, which was there every step of the way. Because TBI is life-altering for the person affected as well as their caregivers, he and his family discovered how cultivating resilience was an important step in moving forward.

They started Love Your Brain to provide a transformative holistic health environment based on their core pillars of community, mindfulness, nutrition, and movement. Their retreats are also designed for TBI caregivers, providing powerful evidence-based programs aimed at encouraging self-empowerment and resilience. We were looking forward to meeting some new people and learning some new things for our own journeys. We were not disappointed.

Sierra and I had a fantastic time doing things we would not normally get to do, like water sports and crafting projects, and we got to meet incredibly resilient and inspiring people who had all overcome so many different challenges but had been brought together for the same reasons.

I was not Sierra's mother or caregiver during this time, but I partner in mindful events, experiences, and emotional discoveries. It was a wonderful retreat, and so unifying for us both to meet other people who had experienced similar situations as us. We discovered most of TBI's caregivers were also family members, usually mothers.

It was cathartic for me, too, to meet and share with others in the same position. We both made some great friends from this retreat, and Sierra is still in touch with many of them. Love Your Brain builds incredible communities. The way they are chipping away at de-stigmatizing brain injuries is wonderful to see. I am so grateful for what they offer and provide.

It was also very inspiring for us. Sierra and I had been working on her own TBI not-for-profit organization to work with TBI patients in a slightly different way. Having just incorporated our nonprofit organization "Unmask the Invisible," it was great to see how these programs had such an encouraging impact and could be so positive.

Over the year, though, she had become increasingly self-conscious about the scar at the base of her throat from having a tracheotomy tube in place for weeks. We were grateful for the life-giving oxygen it had provided her with for so long that she could not breathe on her own. It was an unsightly hole about the size of a quarter, and the scar tissue was noticeably darker than the rest of her neck.

She could also feel it when she swallowed. It didn't hinder her ability to consume food or drink in any way, but it just continually felt like something in her throat. We decided to consult a plastic surgeon about scar revision in early October and discovered that it would involve repairing the windpipe and closing the muscles of the neck over the windpipe.

After an extensive consultation with a plastic surgeon at Dartmouth Hitchcock Medical Center, it was decided Sierra would be a good candidate for such a procedure. Sierra was scheduled for outpatient surgery in November. We were all a little nervous, as she would be placed under general anesthetic to perform the procedure, but it would be quick, and she would not have to stay overnight.

Sierra was excited, though. She would be free from the feeling of something in her throat and the unattractive scar that she was extremely self-conscious about. Surgery day came, and, on that day, the procedure went smoothly, and she was back home by dinnertime.

Several days after the surgery, almost immediately, the scar was flatter and a different shape, and when it healed, it was barely noticeable. It was her final procedure to correct any lasting physical effects from the crash, and she was delighted.

Sierra was doing so well and had resumed going out hunting and fishing with her dad as she used to before the crash. She was elated that they could still do those things together. She was also doing well with her community college courses and had started working at The Home Depot in town.

She now joined the plethora of people from our orange family who prayed so fervently for her recovery and cheered her on with each milestone of accomplishment. We continue to try different therapies with her as we are aware that her brain is constantly strengthening, and we continue to meet inspiring people.

December is a busy time in our home, and 2022 was no different. We now had four immediate family birthdays, soon to be five, to celebrate before Christmas Day, with the added joy of Lindsay's daughter, Ava Reese, whose birthday is also in the first week of the month. She was already one! The girls turned 20 years old the week before Christmas, and Aspen was home from college.

We celebrated the event with a small-ish party at home, although now our family had grown with Lindsay's husband and baby and Tristan's fiancé, plus close friends of the girls and Tanner and Steven's parents, there are usually at least twelve to sixteen people at our small family gatherings. It's always a full house.

As we sat around our festive table that Christmas, watching our family enjoy their time together, the joy was palpable. Steven and I reflected on the previous year, and we agreed that we serve a generous and loving God. The events of the last eighteen months, although at times difficult, had changed our family and extended family for the better.

Our children and granddaughter were healthy and thriving, our extended family was all doing well, and we were part of a kind and gracious community. The power of prayer has taught us all how to live truly in the moment and that God's love can overcome all. You never know the path you have been set to travel on, but we now know with certainty that miracles occur and the power of prayer is real. With God, all things can be faced and conquered.

On December 28th, God blessed us with our grandson, Bowden Arthur. He was born healthy and strong, and we quickly bonded in love.

Our Heavenly Father certainly is to thank for everything in our lives, and for this, we are grateful.

Chapter Fifteen – A Foundation Is Born

[11] For I know the thoughts that I think toward you, says the LORD, thoughts of peace and not of evil, to give you a future and hope. Jeremiah 29:11

It makes sense that different countries follow different medical philosophies, but I had not really been aware of how vastly different they could be until we met a team of Neurotherapists, Speech and Language Doctors, and their students from the University of Essex in England online. They were occupational, speech, and physical therapists who were working with interns and focused on working long-term with young adults who had experienced a traumatic brain injury.

Given Sierra's initial catastrophic diagnosis and her incredible healing journey, they were very interested in what we did to contribute to her recovery and how that unfolded. And obviously, if it was reliably repeatable.

The UK medical community took the lead for years in researching the brain and long-term effects of traumatic brain injuries, even developing the world standard, The Glasgow Coma Scale, to assess consciousness levels in patients in the 1970s. This scale is still used all over the world today and is the accepted means of defining initial brain injury.

They also led the way in defining post-traumatic amnesia (PTA), which is the disorientated and, at times, delusional state a person experiences after a head injury. This can last anywhere from a few hours to months, depending on the damage and length of time the patient was unconscious.

Over the last decade, there have been greater international collaborations that provide important information as countries recognize head injuries and brain trauma for the complex occurrences they are. In almost every country, traumatic brain injury has been the leading cause of injury-related death and disability, costing billions of dollars for years.

As we experienced first-hand, there are so many variables when it comes to the healing of the brain. It is not a simple cut-and-dried process like breaking a bone, as every brain injury is different.

With over 90% of TBIs categorized as "mild" but over half of those patients not fully recovering by six months after the injury, there is still much to research. We were happy to share Sierra's journey with anyone who was interested, whether they were part of the medical community or not, thereby learning more ourselves.

Through a chance meeting online, I started corresponding with Dr Andrew Bateman, a professor from the University of Essex who's specifically interested in a wide range of ongoing rehabilitation and assistive technology and neuropsychological rehabilitation.

I was also interested in talking to him about integration back into the community, as it was an area in which we faced many challenges. From my own research into the different ways each country's social services are set up, I found, much to my dismay, this is where the U.S. is lacking.

Sure, emergency medical treatments are readily available in the U.S. and outstanding in the fact that the initial priority is to save lives, and for this, I am incredibly grateful. But it's the aftercare when the TBI patient needs additional intensive and tailored support to rejoin society that needs awareness and has room for improvement. The philosophy around the psychological and social aspects of a TBI patient is a serious gap that needs bridging.

From my perspective, there are three reasons this transformation is so difficult. The first is that the demand for visible, rapid, and sophisticated emergency trauma care, which is at the high end of technological and rehabilitative medicine, sets the perspective on TBI recovery. By contrast, long-term medical support and lower-level, everyday rehabilitation do not share the same profile in the allocation of resources or funding of research.

I discovered this whole department at the University of Essex is dedicated to the research and support of Neuropsychology and Social Care programs of the brain. There is also an informative organization called Headway, which is a government-funded foundation that provides long-term support, services, and information to brain injury survivors, their families, and caregivers, as well as professionals in the health and legal fields.

With 125 groups and branches across the U.K., Headway is a well-researched and well-funded organization. Here in the U.S., we have The Brain Injury Association of America, but unfortunately, it is not so extensive and supportive (yet).

The second hindrance reflects the need for each TBI patient's specific handicaps to be considered, especially long term, when setting a rehabilitation plan. I've observed firsthand how difficult it is to leave the shelter of the hospital to reenter the "real world."

Notably for those with ongoing mild to moderate cognitive and physical issues because it is impossible to see an injured brain, and these people "look fine" from the outside. The adjustment back to their former lives is slow and painful. Often, their intimate, family, and friend groups may irretrievably fracture, leaving them with little support anywhere. They must confront changes in their personality as well as redundancy due to ongoing disability.

This often results in depression and hopelessness in the patient. Those with severe injuries may never leave residential support care, as there are no structures or support in place to assist them in returning home.

The third reason directly relates to the mental health of the patient. Most of the physical recovery and improvement takes place within the first year after the injury and is easy to measure, as we saw with Sierra, which is the first aim of initial care and rehabilitation. However, the more time that passes from the date of injury, the more prominent the mental health factor becomes.

With cognitive disorders and mood disturbances becoming more obvious, both end up being more important than physical recovery in the long term. The most reported outcome besides the lasting physical disabilities is depression, with a reported 25% of TBI patients being affected. This also contributes to the breakdown of intimate relationships, social isolation, and poor quality of life.

Depression can also carry over to the family, especially the caregiving relatives. There is minimal "hands-on" support for these key players in a TBI victim's recovery, yet they have such a huge impact on the patient's prognosis.

The level of stress experienced by family members of patients who have experienced TBI is such that professional intervention is warranted but not often received. The better family members can cope with the situation, the better the patient's recovery. Support from professionals reduces the stress experienced and encourages people to cope effectively.

While all these things have been identified as areas needing research and resources, progress is slow, and most of the time, it falls on a patient's own family or caregiving relatives to investigate and discover resources that may be available for their loved one.

I am cognizant and grateful that we were able to provide this type of support for Sierra as a family, but my heart aches for the families who do not have such a strong unit to fall back on, especially families that are not close geographically or are on the lower socio-economic end of the community.

Having to work to put food on the table, along with caring for other children and organizing a schedule for the person experiencing the TBI, is often out of reach for many, which leads to a breakdown of the family unit.

We learned first-hand how difficult it could be for a brain-injured person to find the right resources to rejoin society. In fact, we felt this so deeply. It was one of the driving forces behind Sierra's organization and something we are focusing on to unmask the invisible.

Brain Injuries are invisible yet potentially devastating injuries, and without the resources or support to have the opportunity to participate in "normal" life again, it doesn't matter how far a person has come on their healing journey if there are no structures in place to support them as time passes.

As Sierra had experienced, however, the invisible stretched beyond traumatic brain injuries. Bullying and domestic abuse are also invisible traumas that many people deal with. Sierra knew first-hand what it felt like to be bullied.

After her early experience as a fourth grader and then with her ex-boyfriend, she knew very well the feelings of powerlessness and how easy it was to believe lies that are fed to a child/teen/person in a narcissist or predator's quest to control someone else.

Our family also knows how easy it is for something like this to fly under the radar, putting the changes down to regular teen behavioral ups and downs. Wanting privacy, being secretive, and having low self-esteem all fall within the "normal" range of teen behavior.

Bullying is abuse; there is no difference. The fact that the two are treated differently simply due to age and situation does a huge disservice to everyone who experiences such treatment.

Right from the early days of her healing when she returned home from Spaulding, Sierra was concerned to the point of distress for others who were experiencing any type of trauma in their lives. She would ask Steven and me to share stories from friends and acquaintances sent to us through social media so we could pray for them. Despite everything she had been through and was still going through, I was astounded at her capacity for compassion.

She had always loved to draw and paint, and much to her delight and determination, as she recovered, her creative abilities returned. She resumed drawing and painting with ease, which she had always loved.

She would take great care in creating posters and messages of love and support that she would send via social media to other children, teens, and their families experiencing similar adversity. She had also always been a very compassionate and empathic person, but what we were witnessing was at the next level. Her capacity for love and thoughtfulness was evident even as she was still learning the basics of independence all over again.

Steven and I had realized early on that she naturally amplified caring and concern for others, which was more apparent as she recovered from the crash, would be best channeled into a more organized form, that God's purpose for her life was becoming clear.

We agreed that some sort of organization would be a good platform to offer solace, spiritual support, and education to the many people experiencing "invisible" adversity like brain injuries and abuse in their lives. And if we could offer support and education to the families as well, it would enable us to give back in all the ways that people so selflessly gave to us.

It was becoming obvious that we should help others who are struggling and that Sierra's story had the potential to bring hope and comfort to those who felt they had none. Our family had been fortunate enough to experience such an incredible outpouring of love and support from those close to us and strangers so invested in Sierra's journey, which was incredibly uplifting during the darkest moments of indecision and fear. We decided we needed to remain in the support realm ourselves and fully embraced Sierra's wishes to pay it forward.

In 2021, we came up with the idea of a not-for-profit organization. As time wore on and we experienced so many different situations and had to teach ourselves to advocate for Sierra in many ways, we made plenty of notes about who we wanted to reach, how, and what we could offer them. We identified "gaps" in services and support for TBI survivors and their families.

We outlined our goals and missions, and in August 2022, I incorporated the non-profit foundation "Unmask the Invisible." Our mission is to teach resiliency and inspire those adaptively living with Traumatic Brain Injury through education, art, and advocacy.

Our vision is to create a network of lifelong support for TBI survivors, caregivers, siblings, and providers.

By April 2023, we had appointed our talented and dedicated Board of Directors, who are committed to making a positive impact in our communities. Together, we hope to make an impact and illuminate the invisible.

www.unmasktheinvisible.org

Chapter Sixteen – Love Wins

A Psalm of David.

1 The L<small>ORD</small> is my shepherd; I shall not want.

2 He makes me lie down in green pastures;

he leads me beside still waters;

3 he restores my soul.

He leads me in right paths

for his name's sake.

4 Even though I walk through the darkest valley,

I fear no evil;

for you are with me;

your rod and your staff—

they comfort me.

5 You prepare a table before me

in the presence of my enemies;

you anoint my head with oil;

my cup overflows.

6 Surely goodness and mercy shall follow me

all the days of my life,

and I shall dwell in the house of the L<small>ORD</small>

MY WHOLE LIFE LONG.

P<small>SALM</small> 23. (NKJV)

Miracle is not a word we take lightly, yet there is no doubt that Sierra has been touched by many of them, and often since July

2020. From the fact that she even survived the helicopter ride to the hospital to those first days filled with uncertainty, as we sat vigil next to Sierra's bed in PICU, she was never expected to regain any quality of life, let alone play sports or drive again.

Through it all, our instinct was to pray. Doctors and nurses often mentioned our family's devotion to Sierra and the feeling of love and support that surrounded her. We also heard many affirmations along the lines of "whatever you are doing is working, don't stop." Her healing has been incredible, and we are eternally grateful.

There were moments along the way when we could have chosen to fall into despair and futility or bitterness, but when it came down to it, Our Heavenly Father and St. Padre Pio were guiding us and watching over Sierra every step of the way. Making their presence felt and known at pivotal moments, just when all hope seemed lost, placing the right sign, person, or circumstance in the right place at the perfect time for her.

Sierra is not the only one who has been permanently altered from this experience. Every single member of our family (immediate and extended) has evolved into a deeper, more compassionate version of themselves. This has also been commented on by co-workers, teachers, and friends, and as a family, we are closer than we ever imagined. This, in turn, has also given every one of our children a secure base from which to branch out.

I have been touched by the number of people who reached out, supporting us in prayer and even gifts, people inspired by her journey. People we did not know previously. It felt like people were looking for something to give them hope again after the fear and isolation of COVID.

We assembled an army of prayer warriors. You never really know the full impact of your actions and how far-reaching they can be, but prayer united us all, and we divinely felt the energy. We still hear from people through Sierra's FB page, people reaching out and letting us know they have been praying for Sierra from the start and how inspiring her recovery journey has been to them personally.

Although we already were a Catholic family of believers, we have built a closer relationship with the Lord Almighty, and our understanding of how He works has been broadened considerably. We have learned that there are no coincidences that the kindness of strangers can often change the course of your own life and the lives of the people you love. We have met people who have been sent directly from heaven. And some who have not.

Despite everything, the last three years of our lives have brought more depth and richness than I ever thought possible to our family. We have seen and experienced things that none of us could have imagined at the beginning of 2020.

We have learned that God is in control. He speaks to us through people, signs, dreams, and nature.

We have learned that there is no need to question His will or try to take things into our own hands; He sees all. And in the end, the only person you need to be concerned with is you. There is no need for plans of vengeance. It is all in God's hands. This we know to be true.

We have also learned that the true nature of people is revealed in times of great stress and adversity, with the most surprising people becoming diamonds in our lives.

We have learned that prayer and love are powerful forces, and love truly does overcome everything.

We have learned that people can lift each other energetically and direct those intentions through the power of prayer and the spoken word.

Looking back, there were so many motivators that assisted in Sierra's recovery. Certainly, there were character traits, family ties, the support of a massive community, and the right medical procedure or therapy becoming apparent at the right time. Keeping up with her sister, Aspen, especially during their senior year of high school, was without a doubt one of the biggest motivators for her.

But I do think there was one predominant factor that contributed to Sierra's healing success: God answered the many prayers He heard and gave us our miracle. We have been and continue to be divinely guided. The bond the twins share is also stronger than ever. Sierra and Aspen remain each other's biggest supporters. I am grateful that Sierra has always had such a spark for life. She wants to see and experience it all.

Our hope is that sharing Sierra's journey and story with you will multiply hope, inspiration, faith, love, and kindness in the world.

It certainly has been a long road, but the continued prayers, love, and presence are strongly felt and remain evident even to this day!

We will forever be grateful for God's intervention, awakening us beyond this physical world, giving us a chance to show what love can do in the worst of circumstances, and now we are able to pay it forward through her organization – Unmask the Invisible, Inc. We invite you to journey through the website www.unmasktheinvisible.org. There are so many ways to become involved and support others.

We can ALL make a difference and heal the world one step at a time!

A Note from Sierra.

Dear Readers,

I would like to thank every single one of you who purchased and read this book. As an introvert, telling my story has been daunting at times but so necessary. My biggest desire is to offer hope and inspiration to others, and it reminds me that my journey is bigger than the way I feel.

At the end of my junior year of high school, my life changed in a matter of seconds. I always heard about how fast life can change, but until you experience it for yourself, you just don't realize how dynamic that can be.

Ultimately, though, after what I experienced in that coma, I also realized it was up to me to choose how to continue my story. Was I going to give up and play victim? Or give thanks and go for it? I knew I had been given another chance in life, and I decided to go for it.

I hope my story encourages everyone else to give thanks and go for it, too! I think that it's the smallest and most simple things that stick with you and create lasting memories. We should never miss a chance to tell people we love them. Mostly, though, we should take in the small moments, have faith, and believe that God will always come through in unexpected ways.

With love - Sierra

[17] Therefore, if anyone *is* in Christ, *they are* a new creation; old things have passed away; behold, all things have become new. 2 Corinthians 5:17

Testimonials:

"My 8-year-old son saw a couple of posts about Sierra and the signs everywhere for her. We don't normally pray, but at night, before we go to bed, and he and I both said a prayer for her. He was so sad and wanted to help. She is in our thoughts and prayers."

"I know following Sierra's journey and your faith has helped me in my faith. I've always believed in the power of prayer. I've always believed in angels and in miracles. I've always believed things happen for a reason, and oftentimes, we never learn the reason. Following Sierra's journey, seeing so many people praying for her and your family was truly amazing. I love reading the scriptures you've posted. It's so awesome to see such an outpouring of love and prayers and see Sierra's miracle unfolding. God is so good." ~Bonnie Holbrook

"Sierra's miracle has brought me closer to the Father, Son, and Holy Spirit through Jesus's inner peace! Her journey has inspired me since the ride home from the hospital. Her story put me on a much better path. Thank you, Sierra, for being the miracle that you are," ~ Joe Longmoore

"Sierra's miraculous survival from such a horrific injury is remarkable. Her story is incredibly inspirational, but what inspires me most is her indomitable spirit and her desire to change the world. She has every reason to be bitter, yet she is filled with love. I invite everyone into Sierra's journey. It's impossible to know her and not come away happier. The faith and love of the entire Longmoore family is to be admired." ~ Jerry Serra

"I work with Sierra 2-3 times a week. When I see her name on the schedule, I know what kind of day it is going to be. First, I get my hug, and then the day is filled with smiles, giggles, and happiness. When I know I am having a bad day, Sierra senses it and automatically comes over and says, "My Home Depot momma needs a big hug." She makes me melt knowing what this young lady has gone through and still daily struggles. I know I can do what I set my mind to. Sierra is a true inspiration. Some don't understand what she has been through, but that is Sierra's journey to tell them. I know my heart swells and smiles when I get my hugs from her. Why? Because I know they are truly filled with the most unconditional love, and it means the world to me." ~ Lisa Beam

"Sierra's story has been a tool for learning on the subject of TBI injuries. For 30 years, I have enjoyed working with Special Needs children and young adults (God's Angels). I shared your story, Sierra, with my two young ladies, and they always look forward to learning all the things you achieve each day. They worked harder to meet their goals each day as well. Thank you! God does work in so many wonderful ways. I am thankful to you and your family for being a part of mine. Best of Luck, Sierra… You will Persevere." ~ Brenda Clapp

"Amy, you put a voice to your daughter Sierra's Journey through Traumatic Brain Injury, which helped me heal from my own experience when my. Son was fighting for his life from a Traumatic Brain Injury, and there were no guarantees as to his recovery or what kind of life he would have.be able to have, very hard on him and all of us! He had to relearn everything, like brushing his teeth, walking, using his hands, etc., as well as how to go on from a TBI and continue living and working, no small task for sure! I was a Christian, and my Lord Jesus was my strength, light, and love. He carried me and my son through this, had given my son over to Him when I was expecting my son, and have given him over again many times during his life! God loves our children more than we do, and God has only shared them with us to teach, love, and raise them. Thy Will Be Done! Amy, not only did you and others put words to Sierra's Story, but God used you, her, and others by giving Scripture as a mighty testimony to your faith! To God Be The Glory, and I pray that many will come to know Him personally and have Eternal Life through the Lord Jesus Christ! TBI is Real, and I pray for help and awareness for all who suffer, including their families and for all who will be impacted by TBI." ~ Vivian Hovey

"I do not know you or your daughter, but I have been praying and asking all I know to join. My baby girl is eight, and I would have no understanding, but your strength and relationship with God made me open my eyes. I pray to God my children and I get to meet Sierra."

Made in the USA
Columbia, SC
20 January 2024

6bd49d88-c835-40dc-ad30-725631c57545R01